The
SELF-MOTIVATION
Workbook

Adrian Tannock

For Hannah Gray

Adrian Tannock is an experienced therapist and author. He has helped hundreds of people make positive changes to their lives. Adrian also works with elite-level athletes, improving their confidence, determination and performance. This book draws on those experiences; it describes techniques that really work.

Adrian is a passionate writer whose other books in the Hodder Teach Yourself® series include *Beat Insomnia with NLP* (2011), *The Confidence Workbook* (2012) and *Stop Procrastinating and Get Things Done* (2012). His therapy practice is based in Manchester, England.

The SELF-MOTIVATION Workbook

Adrian Tannock

Acknowledgements

Thanks to Gareth Palmer, Ric Moylan and Scott Quigg for their support and encouragement, and to Victoria Roddam for the opportunity.

Contents

How to use this book

This workbook from Teach Yourself® includes a number of special features which have been developed to help you understand the subject more quickly and reach your goal successfully. Throughout the book, you will find these indicated by the following icons.

 Key ideas: to make sure you grasp the most important points.

 Spotlight: an important and useful definition explained in more depth.

 Exercise: designed to help you to work out where you are, where you want to be and how to achieve your goals. Exercises include:

 Writing exercises – fill in your answers in the space provided.

 Reflective exercises – think about the way you do things.

 Dig deeper: an exercise that offers further reflection or deeper explanations of the topic.

 Test yourself: assess yourself with multiple-choice questions or multiple selections.

 Practice: put the ideas you learn about into practice.

 Quotes: inspiring and motivating you.

At the end of each chapter you will find:

 Summary: a section consolidating the main things you should remember from that chapter.

  What I have learned: helping you summarize for yourself what you can take away from each chapter.

 Where to next?: introducing you to the next step.

At the end of the book you will find:

  Appendices: exercises and a record sheet that will help you consolidate and put into practice what you've learned.

1 *What is motivation?*

In this chapter:

▶ you will learn about motivation: what it is, where it comes from and how to improve it

▶ you will learn how to get the most from this workbook and discover the secret of better motivation

▶ you will need: a pen, a portable notebook and an open mind!

→ The force that drives us forward

What is your *motive* for reading this workbook? What do you hope to achieve?

Whatever your motive, it has compelled you to act. You are now 'motive-ated'. Your reasons and objectives have given you impetus – the force that drives us forward. You cannot be motivated without an objective in mind. There *has* to be a reason.

In theory, self-motivation involves three simple steps:

1 Think about your motive for taking action.

2 Feel desire and a willingness to act.

3 Act until your objective is complete.

Of course, life isn't quite this straightforward – there are challenges to overcome. Motivation is easily lost, and people are prone to wasting time. However, learning to motivate yourself is possible. And doing so will change your life.

Self-motivation depends on using certain skills. This workbook explains everything you need to know. You will explore techniques for building desire and focus, and learn how to overcome the challenges we all face.

Your progress will reflect the time you spend practising. As with everything, you get back what you put in.

→ Perspectives on motivation

> *'Action may not always bring happiness, but there is no happiness without action.'*
>
> Benjamin Disraeli

There are many competing theories on motivation – too many to explore here. However, let's consider self-motivation from various perspectives. You will then understand how it can improve.

Motivation gives us impetus. Like all human experiences, it affects us in different ways. Consider the following:

▶ **Motivation changes our thoughts:** we consider what we could do next.

▶ **Motivation changes our emotions:** we feel willingness, desire and intention.

▶ **Motivation changes our behaviour:** in the most obvious sign of motivation, we act towards our aims.

Motivation increases or decreases in strength. Contrast the list above with this:

▶ **Low motivation changes our thoughts:** we avoid thinking about the tasks at hand.

▶ **Low motivation changes our emotions:** we feel inert, frustrated or anxious.

▶ **Low motivation changes our behaviour:** we'll do anything other than make a start.

Low motivation often causes distraction and avoidance; we are compelled to do less rewarding things. Motivation is a question of *direction* as well as strength.

UNCONSCIOUS PROCESSES

Your brain is currently performing sophisticated tasks: controlling your eyes, understanding these words, processing the information you're reading, forming new memories, etc. This activity creates your experience of being you, but it sits beyond your conscious awareness.

You might be aware of your 'voice' in your mind, but you are not conscious of its construction. This is true of most things; your reality is created without your conscious input. In fact, your reality is idiosyncratic and subjective, even though it feels 'real' to you.

Similarly, we are not even aware of our whole mind. Unconscious beliefs, values, hopes and fears are woven through the fabric of who you are. Relinquish any ideas of perfect control or self-awareness. People are complex and contradictory, with hidden depths and irrational rough edges.

Learning to motivate yourself means working with these processes. You cannot just snap your fingers and demand that things simply change. Progress depends on learning new skills, changing your perception and training your brain to think differently.

MOTIVATION AS A PROCESS

We saw how motivation affects us on different levels, changing our thoughts, feelings and actions. Being a process, motivation evolves over time. It ebbs and flows, strengthens and weakens, reacting dynamically to the challenges we face.

Here is how self-motivation looks when mapped across time:

Before action:

▶ *Our thoughts*: we plan our next move and commit to taking action.

▶ *Our emotions*: willingness increases and we feel ready to act.

▶ *Our behaviour*: the moment comes and we take action.

During action:

▶ *Our thoughts*: sometimes focused and sometimes distracted, our thoughts evolve from moment to moment.

▶ *Our emotions*: our willingness may occasionally give way to frustration, but sustained focus should see us through.

▶ *Our behaviour*: even though we may become distracted – depending on our thoughts, our feelings and the challenges we face – we're generally engaged in the moment.

This example describes solid motivation. Notice that it is not *perfect*. The human mind is too complex for that. Our motivation reacts dynamically to the challenges we face, evolving as we progress.

MOTIVATION AND ACHIEVEMENT

Achieving worthwhile goals takes effort and persistence. Low motivation makes this difficult: challenges mount, we become overwhelmed, and eventually we give up entirely. Unchecked, this destructive cycle ruins lives. Motivation only helps when it is aimed in the right direction.

We can learn to direct motivation skilfully. This means creating strong, focused, sustained and repeated motivation. You cannot get fit via one epic gym session. You would need the motivation to attend the gym *frequently*. Only then would you see results.

→ Improving your motivation

This workbook will encourage you to practise new techniques. Follow the instructions carefully and you will learn a number of skills.

▶ **Create a compelling, achievable goal.** We will begin by exploring goal-setting techniques in detail. These initial exercises are vital to your success.

▶ **Avoid demotivating behaviour.** Often the most important step, this skill cuts through the fog of compulsive avoidance.

▶ **Relax through stress.** As you will learn, motivation depends on feeling relaxed *while* striving forward. Mastering this simple skill changes everything.

▶ **Recognize your freedom.** You will learn how to overcome negative mindsets, distorted perspectives and destructive habits.

▶ **Plan your next action.** You will discover how to boost motivation by breaking tasks into smaller chunks.

▶ **Energize yourself.** For reasons we'll explore, goals can be difficult to believe in. You will learn a powerful technique designed to inspire action.

▶ **Take action.** These steps are meaningless unless you *act*. We will explore techniques to get you moving.

▶ **Acknowledge your progress.** It is important to give yourself credit, otherwise self-motivation becomes a meaningless slog.

Learning these small skills improves everything. In time, your brain will automate them. Self-motivation then becomes a powerful habit and, by that point, you will feel firmly in control.

MOTIVATION AND HABITS

Habits crop up frequently in this workbook - they have a significant impact on motivation. Repeat *any* thought, emotion or action frequently enough and your brain eventually automates it. This habit-forming process is important because it overrides our conscious control. People with low motivation usually accumulate several bad habits. Demotivated behaviour then becomes difficult to control.

The exercises in this workbook will create new 'motivated habits' – providing that you engage with them fully. Motivated habits are the secret to focused, well-directed and consistent motivation. Bear this in mind as you progress through this book.

→ Using this workbook

> *'Everything is practice.'*
>
> Pelé

This workbook encourages you to learn practical techniques. Master these new skills and your motivation *will* improve. Some exercises will suit you better than others, but give each one a try.

Be inquisitive

Approach each exercise as an opportunity to experiment. Even if it feels unfamiliar, skipping forward will hold you back. Be optimistic, patient, and keep an open mind. You have nothing to lose.

Take small steps

The best way to learn new skills is to practise them repeatedly. Focus on taking small steps and avoid racing ahead. Give your brain the time it needs to learn. Anticipate failure *and* success. Both count towards progress. With practice, your new skills will become second nature.

Understand your results

Throughout this book, you will be encouraged to make notes. Pull your experiences apart and learn from them. This is especially true for your 'failures'. Consider your results with an analytical eye. Ask yourself: 'What went right? What went wrong? What can I improve in future?' Learn from *failure* and it becomes valuable *feedback*. Resolve to keep going and your progress is guaranteed.

Do things differently

Your difficulties with motivation may be debilitating, but they are also familiar. Changing this means abandoning your comfort zone. This will be too much for some. They will gloss over the exercises and make excuses. Their motivation will not improve.

That needn't be *your* story. With practice, your approach can change. This is too important to leave to chance. Resolve to do things differently.

Persevere

Some people possess strong powers of motivation. Like any ability, it can be developed and strengthened. Nothing is set in stone. It's never too late to learn new skills. There will be wrong turns, backward steps and frustrations ahead. Persevere with the techniques, especially when things go wrong, and you will achieve your breakthrough. Give yourself the best chance possible and *finish what you have started*.

Work in sequence

Work through each chapter in sequence; each one builds on the last. As note taking plays an important role throughout the workbook, have a portable notebook and pen to hand (or electronic equivalent).

Summary

Let's explore what you've learned so far.

▶ Motivation is the experience of having *impetus*. It is reflected in our thoughts, our feelings and our actions.

▶ Motivation is governed by unconscious processes. Improving it means training your brain to behave in new ways.

▶ Motivation is a process. It responds to various factors, e.g. focus, stress, confusion and desire. It can be strong or weak and directed effectively or otherwise.

▶ Perfect motivation is impossible. The human mind is too complicated for that. However, motivation can be powerful, targeted, sustainable and repeatable.

▶ Keep an open mind as you engage with this book. Take small steps and complete the exercises in order.

▶ Motivation is an ability and, like any ability, it can be mastered. Accept the challenge ahead!

▶ You will need a portable notepad and pen (or electronic equivalent).

What I have learned

→ What are my thoughts, feelings and insights on what I have read so far?

_____

_____

_____

Use the space below to summarize any actions you identify as a result of reading this chapter.

_____

_____

_____

_____

Where to next?

 By now it should be clear: engage with the exercises in this workbook and your motivation will improve. Allow yourself the opportunity to learn.

In the next chapter we will identify how better motivation will benefit you. You will explore the nature of time and consequence and identify what needs to change. This way, you can learn to target your motivation effectively. Let's make a start!

② What is your motive?

In this chapter:

▶ you will identify how better motivation could improve your life
▶ you will discover the PERMA model and how it will help you towards 'your best interests'
▶ you will consider the nature of time and consequence and how you might have less time than you think.

→ What do you want to change?

You are reading this book because you want better motivation. You may need to change or boost just one aspect of your life, or your difficulties could be far-reaching. Perhaps, like many, you don't know where to start.

In each case, the exercises in this chapter will help. We'll begin by clarifying your *motives*, so engage with the following exercises fully, even if you already have a goal in mind.

Ask yourself: 'How do I know I lack motivation?'

▶ Are you often frustrated?
▶ Is life passing you by?
▶ Are you struggling with important projects?
▶ Do you feel left behind?
▶ Is life not going according to plan?

The signs of low motivation are obvious. Time is squandered, problems pile up, and opportunities pass us by. Clearly, this needs to change. Let's begin by getting the full picture.

> *'For myself, I am an optimist – it does not seem to be much use being anything else.'*
>
> Winston Churchill

Exercise 1

THE MOTIVATION CHECKLIST

This simple exercise takes one minute. It identifies what you'd like to focus on. Use it whenever you want to identify an area of your life to improve.

 Read through the following checklist and tick any outcome you would like to achieve. Answer comprehensively – even if you have a specific goal in mind. There is space for your own suggestions if required.

'I would like the motivation to...'

Work
Meet deadlines ☐
Start or finish routine tasks ☐
Return or make phone calls ☐
Answer emails and incoming mail ☐
Start or finish difficult tasks ☐
Apply for a new job ☐
Learn new skills ☐
Change my career ☐
Start a new business ☐
_____
_____
_____

Learning and hobbies
Enrol at college or university ☐
Attend lectures ☐
Revise for exams ☐
Start essays or assignments ☐
Attend group classes ☐
Learn a new skill ☐
Join a reading group ☐
Work on a book or dissertation ☐
Start a new hobby or pastime ☐
Learn or improve a language ☐
_____
_____

Health
Change my diet ☐
Start an exercise programme ☐
Stop smoking or drinking ☐
Make medical appointments ☐
Tackle health problems or injuries ☐
Improve personal hygiene ☐
Learn mindfulness meditation ☐
Learn to cook ☐
_____
_____
_____
_____

Friends and family
Make or return phone calls ☐
Start or end a relationship ☐
Contact friends more often ☐
Be more affectionate or communicative ☐
Attend or arrange social events ☐
Discuss problems when needed ☐
Reply to invitations ☐
Go to the cinema ☐
Join a protest group or organization ☐
_____
_____
_____

'I would like the motivation to...'

Household chores

Do daily chores (tidying, cooking, etc.) ☐
Tackle larger chores (cleaning, ironing, etc.) ☐
Spring-clean the house ☐
Go food shopping ☐
Garden or complete DIY projects ☐
Start recycling ☐
Declutter and get organized ☐

_____
_____
_____
_____
_____
_____

Errands

Open mail ☐
Pay bills ☐
Budget my finances ☐
Complete tax returns and other tasks ☐
Make plans for the future ☐
Execute plans when the time is right ☐
Make timely decisions ☐
Commit to new challenges ☐
Learn to drive ☐

_____
_____
_____
_____

How many boxes did you tick? Even if you ticked several outcomes, don't be too hard on yourself. Low motivation is not shameful; it is created by faulty signals in our brain. Ultimately, you can address each item on your list.

Simply accepting the need for change is a big step forward. You can now focus on learning the skills you need. You just need to practise and experiment. Remember the advice from Chapter 1.

Motivation – why bother?

Before we delve too deeply, let's clarify the reasons for improving your motivation.

Life is complicated and challenging. We face numerous obstacles with our health, our wealth, our families and our jobs. Does low motivation add to your problems? That would be reason enough to change.

Beyond these frustrations, consider the missed opportunities. We should take our chances in life, but low motivation often means missing out. Peak experiences pass us by, and all because we couldn't get going.

Better motivation drives us forward. We then achieve more and avoid certain pitfalls. Naturally, this creates happier lives. This may be obvious, but it is easily forgotten when _inertia_ takes hold.

→ Acting in your best interests

This workbook frequently refers to 'your best interests'. This means anything that contributes to your overall wellbeing. Your best interests change according to circumstance. Consider the following examples.

▶ When starved of fun, enjoying yourself would be in your best interests.

▶ If problems are piling up, then exchanging fun for effort would be in your best interests.

▶ If you're stalling on a long-term goal, focusing on that would be in your best interests.

▶ If you're up to date but exhausted, then getting some rest would be in your best interests.

As a general rule, use common sense to find some balance. To aid this, there are guidelines we can call on.

In 2011, psychologist Martin Seligman described five experiences essential for lasting wellbeing. He called it the PERMA model, and it stands for:

▶ **Positive emotion**

▶ **Engagement**

▶ **Relationships**

▶ **Meaning**

▶ **Accomplishments and achievement**

This model represents a road map to happiness. Let's explore each element in more detail.

Positive emotion

Imagine life without satisfaction, hope or gratitude. It would feel like a sequence of 'other people's photographs'. Consider your home life, your career, your hobbies and your friends. What do you savour? What do you take for granted?

Positive emotions are felt at different times: in *anticipation*, while *experiencing*, and on *reflection*. Emotion is vital to motivation. It is easy to be cynical, but without emotion we cannot hope to progress.

Engagement

We feel *engaged* when our interest is captured. As our concentration increases and our focus narrows, we become anchored to the present. Engagement is being 'lost in the moment'.

▶ Engagement is relaxed and focused *doing*.

▶ It occurs naturally when we are absorbed by something.

▶ When we are engaged, even arduous tasks are rendered less unpleasant.

Sustaining motivation is a challenge, especially with boring or difficult tasks. Instead, we can enter *a state of flow*, working contentedly as time flies by. Engagement is pure motivation.

RELATIONSHIPS

> '*No man is an island, entire of itself...*'
>
> John Donne

Humans are social animals, and relationships are key to our happiness. This does not mean accumulating 'followers' on Twitter. We need relationships that mean something.

Research shows that our resilience depends on supportive relationships – especially with our partner, our children, our friends, colleagues and neighbours. Although building good relationships takes effort and compromise, they are vital for our wellbeing.

MEANING

A sense of purpose gives meaning to our lives. It can be derived from our family or job, or by serving humanity in some way. Meaning is a personal perspective.

▶ Meaning is where you find your truth.

▶ It need not be grandiose or spiritual – just relevant to you.

▶ Even supporting your local football team can lend a sense of purpose.

Revile your job as meaningless and you will grow increasingly unhappy. The same is true for each facet of our lives. Without meaning, life becomes hollow and vague. We need a sense of purpose to flourish.

ACCOMPLISHMENTS AND ACHIEVEMENT

Our achievements make us feel good and build our confidence. They needn't be earth shattering – just important to us. Again, it is a matter of our personal perspective.

▶ The greater the accomplishment, the greater is the sense of achievement.

▶ Achievement depends on motivation. Without it, we always fall short.

▶ Our accomplishments tend to be remembered.

With greater motivation, you will achieve more in life. However, wellbeing requires a certain balance. Constantly climbing mountains only makes people unhappy. Neglect rest and play at your peril.

Using the PERMA model in self-motivation

Unearthing life's positives is a significant challenge that requires care, attention and desire – which is why motivation is so important. You can use the PERMA model to target your 'motive' for taking action. This is especially helpful if you're unsure where to start.

Of course, not everything in life can be positive:

▶ Expressing appropriate negative emotion is healthy.

▶ Some tasks are plain boring.

▶ Some relationships will *always* be negative.

▶ Some experiences bring unavoidable hurt and pain.

▶ Constantly questing for meaning would drive you crazy.

▶ Some endeavours will end in abject failure.

However, you can learn to bounce back from negative experiences and savour positive moments. Your happiness and wellbeing will then increase.

→ The importance of rest and play

Two other factors contribute towards your best interests: rest and play.

Without proper care and attention, even the best-engineered car will break down. You are no different! Enjoying your downtime is just as important as achieving goals in life. No matter how motivated you become, ignoring rest and play risks everything.

THE BALANCING ACT

Of course, a perfectly balanced life is impossible. We must focus our attention where it is most needed. There are only so many plates you can spin at any one time. Attempting too much brings it all crashing down.

You *may* know somebody who is fit and healthy, and who always performs well at work; who maintains a loving relationship with their partner and children and makes enough time for their friends (while finding the time to pursue their interests, and while also saving money and contributing to their community and engaging in spiritual pursuits, and so on). However, for the rest of us, something has to give.

The next step involves deciding where to focus. Let's begin by reviewing the important areas of your life. With better motivation, time becomes your ally, and life begins to improve.

GAUGING YOUR LIFE

This exercise takes around 20–30 minutes. The aim is to consider the degree of wellbeing present in your life.

1 Consider each area of your life and think about the experiences it brings. Take your time – there is no need to race through!

The following worksheets refer to different areas of your life and use the PERMA model. (Although listed in order of *typical* priority, they are all equally important to our wellbeing.) Complete each worksheet by describing your typical experiences in that context. Ask yourself the following questions.

In this area of my life...

→ What positive emotions do I experience?

→ What truly engages me?

→ Where are the good relationships?

→ What personal meaning do I find?

→ What accomplishments have I achieved?

2 Consider your answers by thinking about *before, during and after* an experience, for example:

→ the anticipation of time with a loved one

→ losing yourself in the moment while painting

→ the 'buzz' you feel after exercise.

There are no right or wrong answers. Be honest, and give examples that make sense to you. You may feel that your interest in health and fitness lends great personal meaning to your life, or it may bring no meaning to your life whatsoever. If you have no answer to a question, leave it blank – it is all down to you.

3 Finish each section by summarizing your feelings, using a sentence or two in the space provided.

Here is an example to start you off, relating to health and fitness.

Health and fitness	
Positive emotion	*I love the feeling I get after exercising! The buzz, the endorphins. Also, I love to savour healthy food and really enjoy cooking. Plus, I like how I look!*
Engagement	*After a running for a while, I just lose myself and an hour can fly by. I don't even think about it, I'm just in the 'zone'.*
Relationships	*Steve and I both love staying healthy and keeping fit. It gives us something to do together. I'm more confident when I'm slim, which helps me around other people.*
Meaning	*I'm expressing myself by staying fit, and I love talking to others about it. I like having something in common with people at the gym. Exercise is my life.*
Achievement	*I'm proud of the effort I put into staying fit – with a husband and kids it's an achievement, but well worth it. I couldn't live without my exercise!*
Summary	*I am happy living healthily. It gives me a lot of satisfaction.*

This is a very positive report. You may feel similarly satisfied with an aspect of your life, or you might struggle to be this positive.

Here is a less positive example, relating to work life:

Work and career	
Positive emotion	*I like the people I work with.*
Engagement	*None. It's so dull.*
Relationships	*Again, I like the people I work with. And when they ask me about my job, people seem quite impressed. Does that count?*
Meaning	*It's just a job...*
Achievement	*I don't feel any sense of achievement in my work.*
Summary	*I actually hate my job!!*

This report clearly describes a less satisfactory experience. Realistically, we are unlikely to find positive emotions, engagement, quality relationships, personal meaning and significant accomplishment in *everything* we do. This exercise will highlight the gaps.

4 Now it's your turn. Read through the following sections of the exercise and write down your thoughts and experiences. Spend at least five minutes on each worksheet. Carefully consider what you get out of it, even if it seems difficult at first. Remember that if you genuinely have no answer to a prompt, it's okay to leave it blank.

The different areas of your life that you will consider are:

▶ relationships/family life
▶ work and career (or education)
▶ personal organization
▶ health and fitness
▶ friendships
▶ interests and pursuits
▶ personal growth.

For many people, family is the most important thing and the area you will consider first. It can also be the most stressful: the difference between enjoying romantic times versus feeling misunderstood is beyond measure. Psychological wellbeing and familial support are demonstrably linked. The well supported enjoy their jobs more, are less likely to feel anxious, and feel better equipped to handle illness. Families require significant investment but they bring immeasurable rewards.

Don't forget: if you can't think of an answer to a particular part, leave it blank. A perfectly balanced life is unlikely. There *will* be gaps.

Relationships/family life

 Consider the relationships you have with your spouse or partner, your children, your immediate family and your extended family.

Then, describe how you encounter the following experiences in your relationships/family life.

➜ Positive emotion:

_____

_____

➜ Engagement:

_____

_____

➜ Relationships:

_____

_____

➜ Meaning:

_____

_____

➜ Achievement:

_____

_____

➜ Summary:

_____

_____

_____

Work and career (or education)

We spend more time at work than anywhere else, and job dissatisfaction is difficult to live with. Even enjoyable jobs are stressful. Unchecked, work-based stress causes anxiety and even depression.

Work is a fact of life. We need to earn a living, but not at the expense of our wellbeing. It is never too late to reinvent yourself. So, ask yourself: 'What does my job bring me?'

 Describe how your work and career (or education) contribute towards the following experiences.

→ Positive emotion:

_____

_____

→ Engagement:

_____

_____

→ Relationships:

_____

_____

→ Meaning:

_____

_____

→ Achievement:

_____

_____

→ Summary:

_____

_____

Personal organization

Staying on top of things requires consistent motivation – but the rewards are worth it. Managing your home, your finances and your time decreases stress significantly.

 Describe how you encounter the following experiences because of your personal organization.

→ Positive emotion:

_____

_____

→ Engagement:

_____

_____

→ Relationships:

_____

_____

→ Meaning:

_____

_____

→ Achievement:

_____

_____

→ Summary:

_____

_____

_____

Health and fitness

Are you well hydrated? Do you exercise regularly? Are you healthy and trim? Our health is so important, and yet we often lack the motivation to improve it. This is a recipe for future regret.

 Describe how your health and fitness contribute now towards the following experiences.

➜ Positive emotion:

_____

_____

➜ Engagement:

_____

_____

➜ Relationships:

_____

_____

➜ Meaning:

_____

_____

➜ Achievement:

_____

_____

➜ Summary:

_____

_____

_____

The confidence to change

With three more areas to go, let's break for a moment and consider the importance of *confidence*.

Personal change begins by accepting reality. Sometimes this leaves us feeling overwhelmed; despondency and pessimism take over and precious time is lost. However, there *are* things you can do to improve your motivation: it means learning small skills in the right order. There will be challenges – and successes – ahead. You just need to persevere.

You cannot improve anything by waiting; only action will do. Building motivation is easier when those you trust support you. Can you turn to friends and loved ones for help? What support do you have in your life?

The importance of friendships is beyond measure. Whether providing encouragement or simple good times, friendships enrich our lives and cushion us against loneliness and fear. Our relationships with friends sometimes suffer as life gets in the way, and yet our wellbeing depends on them.

Consider the support networks available to you as you fill in the next worksheet.

Friendships

What positive experiences do you gain through your friendships?

→ Positive emotion:

_____

_____

→ Engagement:

_____

_____

→ Relationships:

_____

_____

→ Meaning:

_____

_____

→ Achievement:

_____

_____

→ Summary:

_____

_____

_____

Interests and pursuits

Although fun is essential to our wellbeing, we often allow our interests to slide. Life then becomes stressful and dull. Your interests and pursuits cannot be wisely set aside.

 Consider your interests, hobbies and pursuits, and write down examples of the positive experiences you gain through them.

→ Positive emotion:

_____

_____

→ Engagement:

_____

_____

→ Relationships:

_____

_____

→ Meaning:

_____

_____

→ Achievement:

_____

_____

→ Summary:

_____

_____

Personal growth

We all need to be challenged. Otherwise, how can we grow? When was the last time you pushed yourself to the limits?

 Describe how you encounter the following experiences via personal growth and development.

→ Positive emotion:

_____

_____

→ Engagement:

_____

_____

→ Relationships:

_____

_____

→ Meaning:

_____

_____

→ Achievement:

_____

_____

→ Summary:

_____

_____

_____

How did you get on? Take five minutes to review your answers. Which area(s) of your life are you satisfied with? Which of them need more attention?

With your answers in mind, return to the checklist at the start of this chapter. What new outcomes could enrich your life? Tick any relevant boxes before continuing.

The journey and the destination

Whatever goals you achieve, they should bring some combination of positive emotion, engagement, positive relationships, meaning and accomplishment. Otherwise, why bother? Similarly, you can learn to experience these elements *while* working on the goal. Then you'll enjoy both the 'journey' and the 'destination'. If you can achieve this, your life will become very rewarding.

→ Consequences and time

This workbook encourages you to learn actively. Whether or not you engage with the exercises, you will experience the consequences. For example, avoiding the exercises in this workbook will lead to the following outcomes.

1 You'll miss out on strengthening your motivation.

2 However, you'll avoid the stress of trying new things.

3 Unfortunately, you will remain frustrated by your low motivation.

4 You will continue to experience difficulties and missed opportunities.

Every action (or inaction) counts towards something: more frustration, or less; more achievement, or less; more freedom, or less – the choice is yours. Accepting the challenge of learning means the following outcomes.

1 You'll learn to strengthen your motivation.

2 However, you'll incur the stress of trying new things.

3 Increasingly, you'll feel less frustrated as your motivation improves.

4 You'll arrive at a future with less difficulty and more opportunity.

The consequences could not be further apart. And yet, even now, you may be thinking, 'Makes perfect sense! I'll start properly next week...' The mind often seeks a get-out clause, and the future is a perfect refuge.

STARTING MONDAY...

We may like the idea of personal growth, but the sacrifices can seem overwhelming. As a result, we only commit to *future* action. This feels better because we still have goals, but we avoid the stress of having to achieve them. It may seem like the best of both worlds. In reality it's incredibly destructive.

Putting things off does not mean you are 'lazy'. Strictly speaking, there is no such thing. Laziness is just an umbrella term; it strips away the complexities of self-motivation and replaces it with a simplistic, judgemental label. The reality is more nuanced and profound.

For now, recognize the destruction this causes. The more you delay, the more frustrated you'll become – and the more you'll miss out.

VALUING YOUR TIME

Time is by far our most important resource. Bronnie Ware, author of *The Top Five Regrets of the Dying*, writes: 'When people realize that their life is almost over, it is easy to see how many dreams have gone unfulfilled. Most people had not honoured even half of their dreams and had to die knowing that it was due to choices they had made, or not made.'

We would rarely lack motivation if we truly valued our time. Instead, we imagine the years stretching ahead of us. Unfortunately, life is shorter than you might think.

The following exercise will show you that we really don't have time to waste.

⏰ *Exercise 3*

HOW MUCH TIME DO YOU REALLY HAVE?

This exercise takes five minutes. It demonstrates how limited our time really is.

 Draw a large circle in the space below. Divide it into half, then quarters, and then eighths. Each segment represents a decade in your life.

→ How much time has passed so far? If you're 50, shade in 5 segments. If you're 31, shade in 3.1 segments, and so on... This is the time you've spent already. We spend a third of our lives asleep, so shade in one third of the remaining segments.

→ How many segments remain? Next, shade in half of what's left. On average, we spend 40 years of our lives working, studying, carrying out domestic chores, spending time with the kids, commuting and watching TV. This time is taken.

→ Now – take a long look. How much time is left? Do you actually have time to waste?

This exercise may leave you feeling anxious or despondent. It *is* shocking to see how little personal time we have. The most important question is: what are you going to do with it? Remember: once spent, your time cannot be refunded...

Summary

We began with the question: 'What do you want to change?' The exercises in this chapter may have answered that question. Your wellbeing depends on finding positive emotion, engagement, positive relationships, meaning and achievement in your experiences. It pays to understand this.

Do you see how precious your time is? Ideally, you are left in no doubt. Waiting to act is destructive and pointless – the 'right' time will just never come. Instead, let's focus on the time you have now.

What I have learned

→ What are my thoughts, feelings and insights on what I have read so far?

_____

_____

_____

Use the space below to summarize any actions you identify as a result of reading this chapter.

_____

_____

_____

_____

Where to next?

In the next chapter you will learn about your emotional mind and discover how it causes conflict. From there, we'll explore your needs and values and revisit the question of consequence.

3 The emotional mind

In this chapter:

In this chapter:

- ▶ you will learn about the emotional mind and how it holds the key to self-motivation
- ▶ you will explore the importance of needs and values and how they can help us – or hold us back
- ▶ you will discover how we cause conflict within ourselves, and how it can be avoided.

→ A simple model of the human mind

Exploring the nature of *time and consequences* is inherently motivating. The previous chapter may have inspired in you a sense of urgency, but a simple reminder to 'get a move on' is clearly not enough – otherwise this would be a short book! The human mind is complicated; motivation is not inspired by logic – it is inspired by desire. Let's explore this further.

Imagine that the human mind has three different parts. They function together – sometimes well and sometimes haphazardly. The *strength* and *direction* of your motivation reflect the degree of orchestration between these different 'minds':

- ▶ **The intellectual mind**

    We each possess the ability to *reason*; we have the capacity to 'make sense' via appraisal, differentiation and objective analysis. Although valuable, intellectual thinking does not create motivation.

- ▶ **The emotional mind**

    We also possess another thinking style, based on *emotional perception*. Although less sophisticated than logic, emotional thinking does inspire us to action (and also inaction).

▶ **The habitual mind**

Habits are formed whenever we *think, feel or do* something repeatedly. They unfold with little conscious control, which makes them very powerful. Our habits either help us or hold us back.

These three different minds interact dynamically. Our success in life depends on how we harness them.

THE POWER OF THE EMOTIONAL MIND

> *'The only way you really do this is if you love it. It takes dedication.'*
>
> Andrew Smith

The inspiration to act generally springs from our emotional interpretations. Motivation is drawn from our core beliefs, needs and values; from our prior learning experiences; and from our hopes, limitations and fears. These factors are often unconscious to us. To understand this fully, let's review a case study.

Jamie's story

Jamie, a 35-year-old father of two, had enjoyed an excellent evening with friends. The next day he logged on to Facebook and was dismayed by what he saw – photographs of himself, many of them unflattering. Never thin, Jamie had put on *a lot of* weight in recent years. Although reluctant to admit it, he was undeniably fat. That same morning Jamie resolved to change his lifestyle and lose some weight. He decided to take up jogging, mainly because he loved the outdoors.

That night, before going to sleep (and anticipating difficulty motivating himself), Jamie wrote himself a motivational note, explaining why he should go running. The next morning he reread his note to himself. Here's what it said:

- Jamie – you don't like the way you look. Do something about it.

- You'll feel better when you've lost some weight.

- Exercise releases endorphins – you'll set yourself up for a good day!

Jamie could not deny the logic of this. In fact, he reflected on the sense it made as he drifted back to sleep...

What is going on here? Let's break Jamie's thought process down into recognizable steps.

1 **The intellectual:** that morning, Jamie reread his note and the logic was irrefutable. Unfortunately, logic does not usually inspire action.

2 **The emotional:** at the same time, Jamie's emotional mind also reached a decision. He felt: a) very comfortable in his warm bed and reluctant to leave it; b) pessimistic about his chances – this felt like another false start; and c) averse to exercising – although Jamie liked the idea of exercise, he found the reality of it unpleasant.

3 **The habitual:** leaping out of bed to go jogging would seem unusual, whereas pressing the snooze button and drifting back to sleep felt quite familiar. This habit kicked in as normal, further contributing to Jamie's lack of motivation.

Jamie's low motivation is easy to understand. His desire to stay in bed outweighed his desire to go running. This lack of desire, created by emotional thinking, was further reinforced by his habit of staying in bed. Combined, they conspired against his best interests.

The emotional mind makes decisions based on subjective perception, which is often distorted. Our decision then becomes quite irrational. However, these perceptions seem real enough at the time.

Let's look at irrational behaviour in more detail. The following exercise sheds further light on emotional thinking.

 *Exercise 4*

EXPLORING IRRATIONAL BEHAVIOUR

This exercise takes just five to ten minutes. It will help you explore the reasons behind recent irrational behaviour.

 Think of a time where you behaved in an irrational way. It needn't be anything important, just obviously illogical. Examples include: overeating and feeling sick; spending money you didn't have; falling out with friends over trivial matters; making yourself unnecessarily late, etc.

Describe your experience using the space below. Remember your thoughts, your emotions and your actions. Explain how the experience impacted on your life.

_____

_____

_____

_____

_____

_____

_____

Quickly review your answer. Did you cause yourself difficulty or did you get away with it? What you could have done differently?

→ Unconscious emotional factors

The emotional mind draws conclusions based on *unconscious* emotional factors. Our conclusions might not be rational, but they still create our reality. They feel more real than simple 'facts'. While deciding whether to go running, Jamie's emotional mind considered the following:

▶ **Perception of the environment around him.** Jamie was comfortable in his warm and cosy bed. He felt quite attached to it.

▶ **The actions regularly carried out.** Jamie rarely went jogging. It felt alien to him, making it less attractive – and less likely to happen.

▶ **His skills and abilities.** Lacking the fitness and experience to jog well, Jamie felt discouraged by the idea.

▶ **His core beliefs.** Deep down, Jamie believed jogging would lead to a heart attack. This was not a conscious belief, but it made jogging far less appealing.

▶ **His needs.** We each hold various drives, and they guide our decision-making. Jamie did not possess a strong need for physical exercise, but his need for comfort was profound.

▶ **His values.** Jamie valued pleasure above physical appearance. He wasn't fully aware of this, but it contributed to his thinking.

- **Significant learning experiences.** While still at school, Jamie had developed a hatred of cross-country running. Again, he did not remember this consciously – but his emotional mind equated jogging to those past experiences.
- **His sense of identity.** Considering this list, it is easy to understand why Jamie did not see himself as 'a jogger'.
- **His capacity for stress and frustration.** As a lover of comfort, Jamie found frustration and anxiety difficult to tolerate. This 'frustration intolerance' prompted him to make weak decisions.
- **His predictions for the future.** As mentioned earlier, Jamie felt pessimistic about his chances. He tended to be under-confident about future success, further reinforcing his pessimism.

You can see why Jamie's logic stood little chance. Our decisions often reflect our emotional reasoning, no matter how irrational it might be. For the most part, human beings are not logical creatures.

Read through this list again. Can you identify these elements in *your* decision-making?

→ Inspiring the emotional mind

People usually struggle to motivate themselves, because their emotional mind has other ideas. Building motivation means aligning your emotional understanding with your logical best interests. Let's review two ways to achieve this.

THE IMPORTANCE OF VALUES

Values are simply qualities we hold in high esteem. They guide and inspire us, driving us forward to express our identity. Living true to our values makes us happy, and we suffer when they are forgotten. Values are therefore incredibly important.

Do you know your values? Many people do not. Take a moment to complete the following exercise – you might be surprised by the results.

IDENTIFYING YOUR VALUES

This exercise takes just a few minutes. It identifies the key values you hold in life. When you have identified your values, keep them somewhere visible and look at them daily.

Read through this checklist and tick any box you truly identify with. Be honest – only tick values that resonate with you. Don't tick something because you would like to value it. Complete this exercise quickly; go with your initial feeling. There are extra spaces for your own answers if required.

Table of values

Acceptance	☐	Accountability	☐	Achievement	☐	Adventure	☐
Affection	☐	Authenticity	☐	Balance	☐	Beauty	☐
Belonging	☐	Caring	☐	Challenge	☐	Change	☐
Collaboration	☐	Commitment	☐	Compassion	☐	Competence	☐
Competition	☐	Confidence	☐	Contribution	☐	Co-operation	☐
Courage	☐	Creativity	☐	Curiosity	☐	Decency	☐
Decisiveness	☐	Development	☐	Discipline	☐	Efficacy	☐
Efficiency	☐	Empathy	☐	Excellence	☐	Enthusiasm	☐
Excitement	☐	Fairness	☐	Faith	☐	Flexibility	☐
Forgiveness	☐	Freedom	☐	Friendship	☐	Fun	☐
Generosity	☐	Gratitude	☐	Growth	☐	Happiness	☐
Health	☐	Honesty	☐	Honour	☐	Humility	☐
Humour	☐	Independence	☐	Influence	☐	Integrity	☐
Involvement	☐	Joy	☐	Kindness	☐	Knowledge	☐
Leadership	☐	Learning	☐	Love	☐	Loyalty	☐
Money	☐	Nature	☐	Openness	☐	Order	☐
Partnership	☐	Passion	☐	Patience	☐	Peace	☐
Play	☐	Possessions	☐	Prestige	☐	Progress	☐
Recognition	☐	Respect	☐	Responsibility	☐	Quality	☐
Security	☐	Service	☐	Sincerity	☐	Stability	☐
Status	☐	Success	☐	Teamwork	☐	Tolerance	☐
Tradition	☐	Trust	☐	Variety	☐	Wealth	☐
Wisdom	☐	_____	☐	_____	☐	_____	☐
_____	☐	_____	☐	_____	☐	_____	☐

From the values ticked above, circle the ten that really stand out. Then consider the following.

→ Think of the really important moments in your life. Why were they so valuable?

_____

_____

→ Which values do you especially respect about yourself?

_____

_____

→ Which values do you wish you could change?

_____

_____

Finally, choose the six most significant values from your list. Write them down and keep them visible; do not shut them away! Look at them daily and remember that you are happiest when living by them.

Your values may evolve as you progress through this workbook. Revisit this exercise after a month or two and gauge any changes. For now, try to express your values in your behaviour. Your wellbeing will increase if you do.

With this in mind, quickly review the checklist at the start of Chapter 2. What outcomes did you tick? Ask yourself: will these outcomes bring me closer to my values?

THE IMPORTANCE OF NEEDS

Needs are more visceral than values. We notice when they are unmet, and this plays a pivotal role in motivation. Various human needs have been identified over the years. For instance, each of us needs food, shelter, security, social recognition, love, acceptance, material comfort and entertainment. Fail to meet these needs and you will grow increasingly anxious, frustrated or despondent.

For the purposes of this workbook, we'll consider the following broad needs when building motivation:

- Safety and security
- Rest and recuperation
- Friends and family
- Competition
- Co-operation
- Saving and collecting
- Physical activity and health
- Curiosity or challenge

- Order, comfort and predictability
- Control or self-determination
- Honour and loyalty
- Idealism or social justice
- Love, sex and beauty
- Independence and individuality
- Recognition, status and acclaim
- Approval, acceptance and belonging

(Note: these categories are not mutually exclusive. For example, the desire to live in a clean and tidy house could reflect a need for 'order and predictability' and 'safety and security'.)

Meeting our needs *in positive ways* enhances our wellbeing, but failing to meet them creates negative outcomes. Here are some examples.

The need for physical activity and health

- Meeting this need means feeling satisfied, healthy and comfortable.
- Failing to meet this need could lead to ill health, sickness and discomfort.

The need for order and predictability

- Meeting this need means that you 'know where you're up to'.
- Failing to meet this need could cause stress and frustration.

The need for approval, acceptance and belonging

- Meeting this need means feeling loved, connected and secure.
- Failing to meet this need leaves us feeling rejected and alone.

Our needs evolve according to circumstance; they are personal and sometimes contradictory. As unmet needs create anxiety, frustration or despondency, we sometimes strive to meet them in unresourceful ways:

- We sometimes meet the 'wrong' need at the wrong time, e.g. meeting the need for 'rest and recuperation' when we should be working towards our goals. The resulting conflict weakens motivation.
- We sometimes meet our needs in destructive ways, e.g. meeting the need for 'safety and security' by smoking cigarettes. This leads us away from our best interests.

▶ We sometimes focus too much on external things to meet our needs, e.g. meeting the need for 'recognition and acclaim' by constantly demonstrating our knowledge – rather than feeling secure in our abilities.

 Meeting our needs in unresourceful ways damages motivation.

 Exercise 6

IDENTIFYING THE NEEDS BEHIND ACTIONS

This exercise takes just five minutes. The aim is to identify the needs associated with some of your actions.

 Think of two demotivating things you do. Remember the wasted time and the poor decisions, the recent frustrations and disappointments. Pinpoint the behaviour that derailed you, and consider the potential needs behind those actions. Use the space below to write your answers. Remember that behaviour sometimes reflects more than one need.

Here is an example to start you off.

Behaviour	*Pressing the snooze button and making myself late every morning!*
Needs met	*The need for recuperation, the need for comfort, the need for safety ... and the need for control (I hate having to get up).*

Now fill in your own examples.

Behaviour	
Needs met	

Behaviour	
Needs met	

How does it look? Could you have met your needs differently?

→ Demotivating needs

As you can see, meeting our needs unresourcefully creates difficulty and destroys motivation. Can you relate to the following demotivating needs?

▶ **Safety and security:** this creates difficulty because we avoid taking risks or leaving our 'comfort zone'.

▶ **Rest and recuperation:** this stops us from exerting ourselves and prematurely curtails effort because 'we're tired'.

▶ **Friends and family:** other people's opinions can destroy our motivation, and yet they do not always know best. We might also over-prioritize the time we spend with friends and family at a cost to our personal progress.

▶ **Order, comfort and predictability:** this creates a fear of change, the unknown, making an effort and failure. Nothing is more debilitating.

▶ **Control or self-determination:** motivation fails when we imagine, often erroneously, that we're being 'told what to do' or relinquishing control.

▶ **Approval, acceptance and belonging:** this creates a powerful fear of being judged or rejected, or a strong desire to 'go along with the crowd' at the expense of our hopes and dreams.

Positive personal change means letting go of destructive attachments. Achieving your goals is impossible if your needs channel your desire elsewhere. To gain perspective, ask yourself the following:

▶ What is the 'right' need to meet right now?

▶ How can I meet this need positively?

▶ How can I meet this need myself?

Answering these questions compels us towards our best interests. Identify the 'right' positive need for a particular moment, and look inwardly for the strength to meet it. Anxiety then gives way to self-determination, and positive action becomes much easier.

→ Summarizing values and needs

As we have learned, even (seemingly) trivial behaviour can reflect our deeper, emotional understanding. The importance of your needs and values should now be clear. Working with them improves motivation. Ignore them and you risk further struggle.

Each decision we take counts towards something. With the lessons from this chapter in mind, let's revisit the question of consequences.

Exercise 7

GRASPING THE CONSEQUENCES

This exercise takes five minutes. It helps you fully comprehend the consequences of your actions.

In Chapter 2 you identified certain outcomes you'd like to achieve – e.g. 'apply for a new job' or 'contact friends more often'. Choose one to explore further. (If you bought this workbook with a goal in mind, choose that.) Consider the consequences of *not* achieving this outcome by thinking through the questions below.

1 What will happen (if anything)?

2 How will it feel?

3 What would you miss out on?

4 What would you see and hear?

5 Would you gain anything?

Next, imagine the consequences of achieving this outcome by answering the same five questions

Here is an example to get you started.

Consequences exercise		
	Failing to: find a new job	**Managing to:** find a new job
1	I'll be stuck in this dead-end job (and with my annoying boss)!	I'll have a new job, which would be fantastic.
2	Really frustrating! I'm bored beyond belief at the moment.	Amazing! I need a new challenge.
3	Nothing (except a better job)!	A new experience. New work colleagues. A new boss! Hopefully a pay rise.
4	The same office. The same people. The same routine.	New people – perhaps new friends. Work that I'm more interested in doing.
5	Nothing I can think of.	I'd miss one or two people, but I can still stay in touch with them.

Now use the table below to record your answers.

 Take your time and use your imagination. Imagine putting yourself into the future, and identify what you'd see, hear, and feel as a result of each outcome. The more vividly you think about it, the more you'll grasp the consequences.

Consequences exercise		
	Failing to:	**Managing to:**
1		
2		
3		
4		
5		

Reflect on your answers for a moment.

 Now ask yourself:

→ Which needs or values would I meet by achieving this outcome?

_____

_____

_____

→ Might certain needs or values cause me to miss out on this outcome? If so, what are they? Write them below.

_____

_____

_____

→ Will achieving this outcome make me happier? Explain how here.

_____

_____

_____

Most likely, achieving this outcome will make you happier. *This is your motive for action.* If you reflect this reality in your thoughts, feelings and behaviour, your powers of motivation will improve.

Summary

By now it should be clear: you are governed more by emotion than logic. This is still you – just a deeper, more powerful and less rational part of you. Direct your emotional mind resourcefully and you'll enjoy abundant motivation. Allow it to govern your actions and chaos will ensue.

While working through this book, pay attention to emotionally driven behaviour. Ask yourself: 'Are my needs or values playing a part in this?' With greater insight, you can guide yourself more effectively.

What I have learned

→ What are my thoughts, feelings and insights on what I have read so far?

_____

_____

_____

Use the space below to summarize any actions you identify as a result of reading this chapter.

_____

_____

_____

_____

_____

Where to next?

In the next chapter we will consider your goals, and explore a powerful tool for guiding your emotions. You will create a *compelling future* you can believe in. This fosters desire, direction and purpose.

4 *Your compelling vision*

In this chapter:

▶ you will consider the goals you could work towards using this workbook

▶ you will discover how to energize your emotional mind

▶ you will create a compelling vision statement – a detailed and permanent description of an exciting future you can believe in.

→ Choosing the right goals

Your goals should seem genuinely rewarding. Otherwise, what is the point? For instance, you might like the idea of becoming more organized. It would certainly improve your life. However, sustaining your motivation will prove difficult without a *compelling* reason. Merely liking the idea is not enough.

Achieving goals causes stress, so your motives have to be worth it. In this chapter we will look to the future and create a *compelling vision* that excites you. Dare to dream, and keep an open mind!

> 'If you are working on something exciting that you really care about, you don't have to be pushed. The vision pulls you.'
>
> Steve Jobs

Let's begin with another case study.

Matt's story

Matt, a talented young boxer from Manchester, is considered the brightest prospect of his generation. Gifted, hardworking and confident, he is possessed by just one desire: to become the world champion. This isn't just an idea. It is his deeply held conviction – it guides his every decision. When preparing for fights, his sacrifice is immense. He simply rises, trains, eats and sleeps. Nothing else crosses his mind.

How is such dedication possible? Matt is just a normal young man. While his friends are out drinking and socializing, he'll be tucked up in bed. Every day he meticulously plans his diet, his fluid intake, his training programme and more. To make all of this possible, he has to believe it worthwhile.

Matt's compelling vision of the future comes in two parts. He sometimes imagines winning the world title. Belt held aloft, a beaming smile on his face; the noise, the heat, the cameras, the fans chanting his name... he knows each vivid detail off by heart, and it excites him beyond words. The second part of his dream is more peaceful – and more powerful. He imagines playing with his kids on a warm sunny day, larking around and having fun, again with that smile on his face. At this point, play-fighting with his children, he knows the sacrifice was worthwhile.

This is not just a pleasant daydream. He feels *compelled* to make it real. It sits at the back of his mind – energizing and galvanizing him, creating his direction and purpose.

Matt's compelling vision inspires his emotional mind. Here's how it works:

▶ **Perception of the environment around him.** Matt is dissatisfied with his current environment. He wants to live in the world of a champion, and he will do anything to make that happen.

▶ **The actions he regularly carries out.** Matt is used to training, competing and making sacrifices. A mere ten-mile jog feels like coming home!

▶ **His skills and abilities.** Matt knows he has the right skills, and this knowledge brings him confidence and determination.

▶ **His core beliefs.** Deep down, and in no uncertain terms, Matt believes he is destined to be a world champion. This belief energizes him whenever he is tired, sore or discouraged.

- **His needs.** Matt has a strong need for recognition, status and acclaim. Only winning the world title will do.

- **His values.** Matt lives by certain values: adventure, growth, challenge, prestige and success. He enjoys expressing these qualities in his actions.

- **Significant learning experiences.** Throughout his career, Matt has experienced the benefit of hard work. These invaluable lessons contribute towards his work ethic.

- **His sense of identity.** Matt views himself as a champion in waiting. This is his identity; it guides his thoughts, his feelings and his actions.

- **His capacity for stress and frustration.** Given that boxers are often punched in the face, Matt possesses a well-developed capacity to handle stress and frustration.

- **His predictions for the future.** Matt holds an optimistic view of his future. He imagines life turning out well – providing he works hard each day.

Can you see why Matt is so motivated? His dream reflects his needs and values; his identity; and his experiences and beliefs. He has confidence in his ability. His compelling vision inspires desire. Matt still has to plan and set goals. He still needs to drive through tough challenges. However, he never debates with himself: 'Should I do the work?' There is only one possibility. His energized emotional mind drives him forward.

Of course, Matt's compelling vision is an extreme example. Yours needn't be so grandiose. However, you must believe that your efforts will be worth it; otherwise, you will struggle to feel inspired.

→ What is your goal?

To get the most from this workbook, you need to set yourself a clear goal. To begin, we will choose something that allows you to practise the techniques in this workbook.

- Do you have a deadline approaching?

- Do you have a problem that urgently needs solving?

- Is there something you've wanted to do for a long time?

- Did Exercise 2, 'Gauging your life', in Chapter 2 highlight an area to focus on?

- What do you want the most?

Ideally, your first goal will be something you can spend periods of time working on, preferably on a daily (or near-daily) basis. This might be, for example, studying, building something, writing or going to the gym. If possible, choose a goal you can complete within a three-month period. We'll look at longer-term goals in Chapter 14.

 In Chapter 5 you will learn more about setting goals, but for now it is better to set an 'approach goal' such as learning a new skill, rather than an 'avoidance goal' such as quitting smoking. (You'll need to develop your skills before tackling avoidance goals.) Ideally, choose something that allows you to refer to this workbook and make notes. Once you achieve this first 'practice goal', you can always define a second one. We'll revisit this in Chapter 14.

If necessary, reread the checklist and consider your answers to Exercise 2 in Chapter 2. If you have a big goal in mind – e.g. graduate from university – break it down into smaller steps – e.g. pass the next three months of the course.

Here are some ideas to consider:

▶ Improve your marks at college or university.
▶ Declutter your home and complete DIY projects.
▶ Change your job or become self-employed.
▶ Learn to meditate.
▶ Organize yourself (errands, chores, finances, etc.).
▶ Learn a new language.
▶ Improve your performance at work.
▶ Get fit and healthy.
▶ Take up a new sport or hobby.
▶ Learn a musical instrument.

What goal do you have in mind? Write it in the space below.

The 'practice goal' I am working towards is:

_____

_____

_____

Remember: motivation requires a 'motive'. Getting the most from this workbook means working towards a goal. Choose just one goal to begin with. Attempting too much will leave you overwhelmed, so take things a step at a time.

Next, we'll explore the compelling vision associated with your goal. The following exercise is *vital* to your motivation.

 *Exercise 8*

CREATING YOUR COMPELLING VISION

This exercise takes five to ten minutes. It connects you with your compelling vision for the future. Use this exercise whenever you're setting a goal.

 Consider your goal for a moment. What will it bring you? What are the outcomes? How will you benefit?

Explore this further by closing your eyes and imagining those outcomes vividly. Really involve yourself in it. Suspend your disbelief and pretend it is actually happening. Then ask yourself:

→ What do I see, hear, and feel?

_____

→ What have I gained?

_____

→ What opportunities will come of this?

_____

→ What needs does this meet?

_____

→ What values am I living?

_____

→ What PERMA model elements am I experiencing?

▶ Positive emotions?
▶ More engagement in my life?
▶ Better relationships?
▶ A sense of personal meaning?
▶ Accomplishment or achievement?

→ How do I feel about myself?

_____

→ What external rewards will I receive?

_____

→ What problems have I avoided?

_____

→ Who am I now?

_____

Repeat this process several times to answer these questions fully. Relax into it and gauge how it makes you *feel*. Motivation is all about emotion.

What emotions emerge? Happiness? Relief? Achievement? How strong is that feeling? Strong? Moderate? Weak? Do you feel anything at all?

What do you like about this goal? What opportunities does it create? How does it relate to the PERMA model, your values or your needs?

The key question is: does this goal feel compelling to you? How much desire does it create?

Connecting with our emotions takes practice. Suspend your disbelief and try to 'act it out' – even if that doesn't come naturally. Aim to make it feel real. Remember to focus on the outcomes.

Sometimes this may seem unnecessary; after all, what is compelling about doing the housework? However, spending time in your lovely clean house *should* feel compelling (providing you actually desire it). Goals needn't be grandiose to feel rewarding.

If you cannot feel any connection, check whether you believe the goal is achievable. Give yourself permission to pretend you're achieving it. If that still does not work, try this simple contrasting exercise.

Exercise 9

CONTRASTING FUTURES

This exercise takes just a few minutes. It connects you to your compelling vision for the future. This exercise helps whenever you feel disconnected from your goals.

Begin by asking yourself: what am I trying to move away from? Spend 60 seconds acknowledging the circumstances you want to change. Be thorough and honest. Note your emotional responses; you should feel some degree of dissatisfaction.

Keeping that dissatisfaction in mind, redo Exercise 8, 'Creating your compelling vision'.

→ How does it change your emotions? Contrasting your goal with your present circumstances should highlight the rewards it will bring.

_____

→ Finally, come back to reality. This goal hasn't yet been achieved. Do you now feel a sense of desire?

_____

Ask yourself:

→ Why do I want this?

_____

→ Is it for me or for somebody else?

_____

→ Do I believe I can do it?

_____

Contrasting current circumstances with positive future outcomes should reveal the point of taking action. If you still feel very little, and you believe the goal is possible, it may not be the goal for you.

At the very least, achieving your goal should bring a sense of relief. Otherwise, although you might like the idea, it's perhaps just not compelling enough. Consider choosing something else.

→ The importance of writing things down

Over the next few chapters we will create several important documents. Together, they form your blueprint for success. These documents are listed below.

Document	Description
1 Your compelling vision statement	This is an emotion-based description of your goal. It answers the question 'What's in it for me?'
2 A SMART goal definition	This is a technical description of your goal. It considers various factors, e.g. the measurable outcomes you hope to achieve and the deadline placed on it.
3 Your action plan	This is a list of the tasks you'll need to achieve to accomplish your goal.
4 Your goal-time calendar	This is an overview of the time available to work on your goal.
5 Your motivation fact sheet	This is an overview of the challenges you face, e.g. the thoughts, emotions and behaviours that weaken motivation.

These documents will keep you on track. Ideally, pin them up where you can see them. If that is not feasible, gather them together in a folder and look through them daily. Hiding these documents away detracts from their usefulness.

Getting things in writing is vital for the following reasons:

1 It shows you mean business.

Achieving goals requires commitment. Writing them down helps.

2 It forms a permanent record.

Goals involve too much information to keep solely in your head. Safeguard your insights by writing them down.

3 You become accountable to yourself.

This stops us extricating ourselves from our commitments.

> It's important to follow all the steps in this chapter. Skipping them will only cause you unnecessary problems later.

YOUR COMPELLING VISION STATEMENT

Our aim with this document is twofold. Firstly, we answer the question: 'What's in it for me?' This creates an important reference point for the future.

Secondly, we will write this statement *as if it were happening now*. This fosters belief and inspires our emotional thinking. Write your answers in the present tense, e.g. 'I am proud of myself', rather than 'I will be proud of myself.'

Here is a compelling vision statement written by Jamie, the reluctant jogger described in Chapter 3.

My compelling vision statement

It is 1 November, and I am fit, trim and healthy.

What am I doing? What am I seeing, hearing, feeling?

I'm entering the final leg of a five-mile jog. It's a crisp morning, nice and quiet. I see the road stretching out in front of me. I'm feeling achy but happy to have exercised.

What have I gained? What opportunities will come of this?

My fitness and self-respect. I'm even thinking of running longer distances for charity – something I would NEVER have thought possible!

What needs have I met, and how do I know this?

1 Physical activity – jogging is certainly that!

2 Good health – I've already lost two stone of fat.

3 Challenge – it's tough but I'm mastering it.

4 Control – I can feel myself toughening up.

5 Recognition – people comment on the weight I've lost.

6 Approval – I don't feel so embarrassed by being fat.

What values am I living?

Competence, commitment, health, discipline, growth, progress.

The PERMA model:

1 Positive emotion: I am relieved not to be as as I used to be. I feel proud of myself. I enjoy the buzz after jogging.

2 Engagement: I like how it feels when I lose myself in running. After a while I just zone out and put one foot in front of the other.

3 Relationships: I feel more confident now that I have lost weight.

4 Meaning: N/A

5 Achievement: It feels good to have set myself a goal and achieved it.

How do I feel about myself?

Really proud, especially because I am losing weight. Healthy, less wheezy.

What external rewards have I earned?

People are definitely treating me with more respect – which I like.

What problems have I avoided?

Three main things: I am healthier, so I worry less about ill health later in life. I am slimmer, so I don't feel so shy, and I feel more determined, which has boosted my self-respect. I hadn't realized I was so negative about the future before.

Who am I now?

I am still just me! Just a happier, slimmer me.

Jamie has really entered into the spirit of things. To fire up his imagination, he talked to friends about their fitness regimes and read about people's experiences online. This helped him when considering his answers. Notice also how Jamie used the present tense. This makes it feel more real.

Now it's your turn. Take your time with this. Read around the subject first, and find out what it feels like to achieve goals such as yours. Seek out other people's experiences (the Internet may be a good place to start).

When you complete this exercise, be thorough and do some research. Work out how your needs will be met, what positive emotions you'll feel, and so on, and use the present tense as in the example above.

Exercise 10

WRITING MY COMPELLING VISION STATEMENT

This exercise might take anything up to an hour. It clearly defines your compelling vision – the point of achieving your goal. Use it when you need to define any goal.

Using your notebook (or a new Word document), write the following heading at the top of the page: 'My compelling vision'.

State a future date (when you have achieved your goal), and describe the experience using the present tense. For example:

▶ It is 30 February and I have finished renovating the house.

▶ It is 25 March and I have just submitted my dissertation.

▶ It is 1 December and I have just handed in my notice at work.

Next, work your way through the following questions, using the spaces below to note your answers. The questions are phrased as if you have *already achieved your goal*. Take your time, consider your answers carefully and be as thorough as possible. You can refer to Jamie's example if you get stuck.

 Using the present tense, describe achieving your goal. Explain what you see, what you're doing, and how it makes you feel. This is your compelling vision in a nutshell.

→ What am I doing?

_____

→ What am I seeing, hearing and feeling?

_____

_____

_____

How has your goal improved your circumstances? What opportunities have you created? As with all of these questions, answer in the present tense.

→ What have I gained? What opportunities will come of this?

_____

_____

Tick which needs your goal has met:

▶ Safety and security	☐	▶ Control or self-determination	☐
▶ Rest and recuperation	☐	▶ Honour and loyalty	☐
▶ Friends and family	☐	▶ Idealism or social justice	☐
▶ Competition or co-operation	☐	▶ Love, sex and beauty	☐
▶ Saving and collecting	☐	▶ Independence and individuality	☐
▶ Physical activity and health	☐		
▶ Curiosity or challenge	☐	▶ Recognition or acclaim	☐
▶ Order, comfort and predictability	☐	▶ Approval, acceptance or belonging	☐

→ How has achieving this goal met these needs?

_____

_____

_____

Which values have you expressed or lived up to by achieving this goal?

→ What three values am I living?

_____

_____

_____

Has this goal connected you to these positive human experiences?

▶ Positive emotion	☐	▶ Meaning	☐
▶ Engagement	☐	▶ Achievement	☐
▶ Relationships	☐		

→ How has achieving this goal connected me to these experiences?

_____

_____

_____

Has achieving your goal improved your relationship with yourself? Perhaps you will feel proud, confident and capable. What else?

→ How do I feel about myself?

_____

What external rewards will you receive (e.g. money, material possessions, travel)?

→ What external rewards have I earned?

_____

Had you failed to achieve this goal, what difficulties would you have faced? What opportunities would you have lost?

→ What problems have I avoided?

_____

Has this goal changed your identity? You may seem very different or not changed one bit! There is no right or wrong answer.

→ Who am I now I have achieved this goal?

_____

How did you get on? Transfer your answers to your 'compelling vision statement'. This is the foundation for your future motivation. Spend as long as you need on it to get it right.

Reading through this statement should spark some emotion. Otherwise, it is just an abstract idea. Before moving on, reread it and ask: 'If I knew I couldn't fail, how much would I want this?' At the very least, you should feel a sense of relief.

Summary

 In this chapter you considered the goals you could work towards using this workbook. You then practised creating a 'compelling vision statement'. This goal should seem genuinely rewarding. Merely liking the idea is not enough.

Over the next day or two, reread your compelling vision statement and fire up your emotions. Believing in the future is a skill, and it might not come naturally. However, motivation requires a motive. Try to connect emotionally with yours.

What I have learned

→ What are my thoughts, feelings and insights on what I have read so far?

_____

_____

_____

Use the space below to summarize any actions you identify as a result of reading this chapter.

_____

_____

_____

_____

Where to next?

 In the next chapter we will turn your compelling vision statement into something concrete, by setting a 'SMART goal' and devising an action plan. By then you will know your goal inside and out. This is how motivation is forged.

5 Setting well-formed goals

In this chapter:
▶ you will learn about SMART goals and how they help build motivation
▶ you will review another case study and see goal setting in action
▶ you will create an action plan – your roadmap to success!

→ Defining clear goals

In the previous chapter you decided on a goal to focus on. Now we will define that goal in thorough terms. Even if you've read about goal setting elsewhere, complete the exercises in this chapter. Your future success depends on it.

Clearly defined goals improve motivation. We know what we're aiming for, and that fosters focus and accountability. Backtracking becomes less likely.

Some people refuse to write their goals down. They imagine it's a waste of time. This reluctance usually reflects a deep-seated fear of failure. Written goals are too great a commitment. Unfortunately, ill-defined goals are easily forgotten and failure then becomes more likely. Do not fall into that trap.

SMART GOALS

Well-defined goals have to be comprehensive. To achieve this, we'll use the SMART goal system. There are different versions, but here SMART stands for specific, measurable, attainable, relevant and time-based. Let's go through each point in more detail.

Specific

Well-set goals specify useful detail. The following examples are too general:

▶ I am going to learn how to cook.
▶ I am going to lose weight.

- ▶ I am going to do more DIY.
- ▶ I am going to become self-employed.
- ▶ I am going to learn Spanish.
- ▶ I am going to become more organized.

These nebulous goals lack focus and would be easy to abandon. Instead, solidify your aims by considering the following questions:

1 What will you see, hear or feel when you achieve your goal?

2 What do you need to do (or not do) for your goal to become reality?

3 What will you gain or lose?

4 Where will you achieve this goal?

5 Who will you achieve this goal with?

6 When will you work towards your goal?

These questions add rich detail to your goal. Contrast the previous examples with the following:

- ▶ I am going to learn how to cook the following meals: chicken curry, spaghetti bolognese, chilli con carne, black olive risotto, and steak and chips.
- ▶ I am going to lose weight by exercising four times a week.
- ▶ I am going to refit the bathroom.
- ▶ I am going to become a self-employed nutrition therapist, with a steady client base, a popular blog and a weekly guest slot on local radio.
- ▶ I am going to learn how to speak Spanish in time for my holiday by taking weekly private lessons and attending night school.
- ▶ I am going to become more organized by decluttering my home (and keeping it that way), learning how to manage my time well, and tracking my finances.

These definitions are better because they describe what is going to happen – and how.

Let's make a final adjustment. Optimize your goals by following these rules:

1 Use action-orientated language.

2 State goals in the present continuous tense.

3 Avoid negative language.

For example:

- ▶ I am learning to cook the following meals: chicken curry, spaghetti bolognese, chilli con carne, black olive risotto, and steak and chips.

- I am getting fit by going to the gym four times per week.
- I am refitting the bathroom.
- I am becoming a self-employed nutrition therapist, with a steady client base, a popular blog and a weekly guest slot on local radio.
- I am learning how to speak Spanish in time for my holiday by taking weekly private lessons and attending night school.
- I am organizing myself by decluttering my home (and keeping it that way), learning how to manage my time well, and tracking my finances.

'I will' goals are fixed in the future. 'I am' goals describe the present moment. Also, notice how 'lose weight' has become 'getting fit'. Positively stated goals work better with emotional thinking.

Glance through your compelling vision statement. Using positive, action-orientated language and the present continuous tense, how would you describe your goal?

Measurable

Your goal may involve working towards a single outcome, e.g. writing a 20,000-word thesis. However, this might require you to achieve multiple aims: compiling your research, writing the thesis, editing it down, etc. Even 'single outcome' goals can be broken into component parts.

What will you have to do – either once or repeatedly – to make your goal happen? Ask yourself:

- How will I identify progress?
- What will I do more (or less) of?
- What milestones do I need to reach?
- What habits do I have to establish – or let go of?
- What will change? What will I gain?
- What problems will I resolve?

For example:

I am learning to cook the following meals: chicken curry, spaghetti bolognese, chilli con carne, black olive risotto, and steak and chips because...

- I go shopping for new ingredients on Mondays and Thursdays.
- I attempt a different recipe four times during the week and once on Sunday.
- I am no longer suggesting eating takeaway every night.
- My cooking is improving.
- I am confident enough to invite my family for dinner – which I'll cook!

I am becoming a self-employed nutrition therapist, with a steady client base, a popular blog and a weekly guest slot on local radio because...

- I am seeing clients.
- My brother-in-law has built my website and designed some business cards.
- I have found an office.
- I have contacted everyone from my nutrition course.
- I am a member of local networking groups, regularly attending their meetings.
- I am insured to practise.
- I am ready to hand my notice in at work!
- I feel ready to approach the local radio station to propose a guest slot.

The SMART goal method sometimes creates duplication, as here: 'I will have a guest slot on local radio' and 'I'll feel ready to approach the local radio station to propose a guest slot.' However, this thoroughness will pay off – you will know your goal inside out.

 Goals differ in their orientation, scope and structure:

Approach goals involve moving towards something, e.g. improving your health, completing a project or learning a new skill.

Avoidance goals involve bringing something to an end, e.g. stopping smoking, lowering stress or taking on less work.

Finite goals have an endpoint in mind, e.g. a refitted bathroom.

Continuous goals usually describe a shift in lifestyle, e.g. becoming more organized or getting fitter. Ideally, there is no endpoint.

Task-based goals involve filling up chunks of time with activity, e.g. writing an essay or learning a new skill.

Habit-based goals are focused on carrying out small, repetitive tasks at certain points of the day, e.g. staying hydrated by drinking plenty of water.

Decision-based goals require us to make consistently motivated decisions. To some extent, all goals are decision-based.

Is your goal task-based, habit-based, or a combination of the two? It will affect the way you plan it. Generally, approach goals are more effective than avoidance goals. If you want to give up smoking, for example, reframe it by focusing on 'becoming healthier'.

 This workbook describes how to *sustain motivation* because people find that the most challenging. If your goal involves completing quick tasks or making motivated decisions (habit- or decision-based goals), you'll be shown how to adapt the techniques to suit.

Attainable

Well-formed goals should extend our ability without exceeding it. Impossible goals are pointless; be realistic and set something challenging yet attainable. Consider the resources you'll need to achieve your goal: space, time, equipment and help from other people. For example, 'I am becoming a self-employed nutrition therapist, with a steady client base, a popular blog, and a weekly guest slot on local radio because I have:

▶ an office (including office furniture)

▶ my brother-in-law's help (for my website and business cards)

▶ contact details for local networking groups

▶ practitioner insurance.'

Success is a journey of many small steps. If you ensure that your goal is realistic and identify the resources you need, over time even huge goals become possible.

Relevant

Does your goal fit the narrative of your life? To a large extent, your compelling vision statement answers this question. Only relevant goals are compelling. Often, it is a question of timing. You may yearn to change your job, and this goal could be relevant. However, there might be problems to address first: financial difficulties or a failing relationship. Relevant goals are usually the most pressing.

For the purposes of this workbook, your chosen goal should allow you to learn new skills *and* bring rewards to your life. If your home is spotless but you're three months behind on that novel, focus on your writing! Anything else would be missing the point.

Time-based

Without deadlines, goals remain just fanciful daydreams. Setting realistic deadlines takes practice. Unrealistic timeframes create too much pressure, but *too* much time destroys urgency and focus. Be realistic while setting yourself a challenge.

For *continuous* goals, such as becoming fitter, deadlines describe the point when everything feels stable, dependable and familiar.

 Well-formed goals *must* be written down. They then become real and tangible. This step is too important to gloss over – you risk losing motivation otherwise.

To see SMART goals in action, let's review another case study.

Owen's story

Owen, a project manager from Bristol, was *famously* disorganized. He was continuously late and forgetful. This became a running joke, one he secretly despised.

Although well regarded at work, Owen's disarray caused serious problems. He often ran late for meetings, and sometimes forgot about them altogether. He dreaded checking his emails each day. They just seemed to pile up uncontrollably.

In many ways, Owen was competent and determined. However, for some reason he'd never learned the value of personal organization. After receiving a dressing down from a senior colleague, he decided things had to change.

To begin, Owen defined a SMART goal using a goal worksheet, shown opposite.

It shows that he has:

▶ clearly defined his goal

▶ determined the outcomes he wants to achieve

▶ listed the resources he'll need

▶ explained why the goal is relevant

▶ set a realistic deadline.

His goal is thoroughly defined. He knows what he wants and how long it will take. All he needs now is a plan. We'll discover how he managed that later.

'*Before anything else, preparation is the key to success.*'

Alexander Graham Bell

In the next exercise we'll turn our attention to *your* goal.

Owen's goal worksheet		
Smart goal	Why it's smart	Definition
Specific	*What is your specific goal (stated in positive terms, using the present continuous tense)?*	*I am becoming more organized at work.*
Measurable	*How will you know when you are reaching / have reached the goal?*	*I answer all emails and voicemails within 24 hours.* *I use an electronic calendar to track appointments, meetings and important dates.* *I use a daily to-do list, adding everything to it and working through it methodically.* *I set time aside each evening to tidy my desk.* *I have an organized filing system for reports, information, etc.*
Attainable	*What resources (equipment, facilities, assistance, etc.) do you need?*	*A proper filing system, and somebody to show me how to use it.* *A good book on time management.* *An 'in-tray' system.* *An online calendar I can access from my phone.* *An organized office!*
Relevant	*How is this goal significant to you?*	*I want to be better organized because I am sick of people making fun of me, of being late constantly, and getting into trouble at work.* *I'll feel less stressed and anxious.* *I'll probably be promoted if I stop making silly mistakes, meaning more money.* *Then I'll be able to afford to buy a house with my girlfriend.*
Time-based	*When will you reach this goal?*	*I can achieve this within eight weeks.*

Exercise 11

SMART GOAL SETTING

This exercise takes 15–20 minutes. The aim is to define a thorough goal you can work towards. Use this exercise whenever you need to set goals, no matter how small.

In the previous chapter you decided on a goal to work towards. Next, consider the questions that follow the worksheet. Have your compelling vision statement to hand.

 Write your answers in the worksheet below. Do not skip this step! Committing to your goal in writing is vital. Take your time. Refer to Owen's example above if you get stuck.

Your goal worksheet		
SMART goal	Why it's SMART	Definition
Specific	*What is your specific goal (stated in positive terms, using the present continuous tense)?*	
Measurable	*How will you know when you are reaching/have reached the goal?*	
Attainable	*What resources (equipment, facilities, assistance, etc.) do you need?*	
Relevant	*How is this goal significant to you?*	
Time-based	*When will you reach this goal?*	

How can you state your goal using positive, present tense, action-orientated language?

What measurable outcomes are associated with your goal?

→ How will you identify progress?

→ What will you do more (or less) of?

→ What milestones do you need to reach?

→ What habits do you need to establish – or let go of?

→ What will change? What will you gain?

→ What problems will you solve?

→ Do you need specific equipment or facilities, or external help?

→ How is this goal relevant to your life?

→ How long will it take to achieve your goal?

How does this goal make you feel? Excited? Anxious? Sceptical? Before continuing, scan through your compelling vision statement and see how the two documents fit together:

▶ **Your compelling vision statement** describes how this goal meets your needs, expresses your values, provides rewards and (potentially) grants you positive emotion, engagement, positive relationships, meaning or achievement.

▶ **Your SMART goal definition** is a technical description of your goal, specifically detailing the measurable outcomes, attainability, relevance and timeframes and deadlines associated with it.

Together, these documents illustrate what you're trying to achieve – and why. Next you need to work out how to make this possible.

→ Creating an action plan

Achievement depends on action, which means knowing the steps you must take. Otherwise, motivation would give way to confusion. To counter this, we need an action plan.

Previously, we saw how Owen defined his goal to 'become more organized at work'. To make this happen, Owen created an action plan. Here is how he did it.

LISTING EVERY STEP

Owen started with a blank piece of A4 paper. He wrote his goal in the middle of the page, like so:

> BECOME MORE ORGANIZED AT WORK

Referring to his SMART goal definition, Owen then asked himself:

▶ What must I do for this to happen?

▶ What tools do I need?

▶ What habits do I need to get into?

▶ What do I have to stop doing?

Owen thought about achieving his goal: sitting at his tidy desk, answering emails and voicemails promptly, keeping track of his appointments, filing things away, and so forth. As he did so, he wrote down the actions required to make those outcomes happen.

After ten minutes or so, Owen's sheet of paper looked like this:

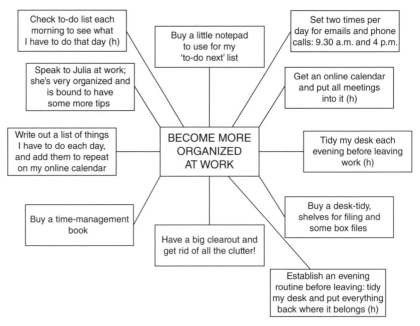

Items marked (h) on Owen's action plan diagram are habits – small tasks to complete regularly.

ORDERING THE TASKS

Owen then rewrote these tasks into a list format, breaking them down further as necessary. Occasionally new ideas sprang to mind, so he noted those as well. This created a comprehensive list, encompassing every task he could think of:

Owen's action plan list	
Action	**Tasks**
1 Get an online calendar (with a reminder function I can access via my phone).	Add times for checking voicemails and emails twice each day. Draw up a list of repetitive tasks and add them into the calendar on 'repeat'. Use the calendar to record meeting times, etc. Add a reminder to check my to-do list each morning. Add a reminder to tidy my desk each evening.
2 Buy a little notepad for the to-do list.	There are A6 notepads in the stationery cupboard; I'll collect one from there. Keep it with me and remember to use it whenever anything crops up. Get a desk-tidy as well.
3 Order shelves and box files for the office.	Make sure I get the right ones (check with Julia). Order with Purchasing. Order a new chair and laptop stand while I'm at it. (Find out who the health and safety officer is and ask for chair recommendations.)
4 Clear out the office.	Sort through old papers, documents, etc, and archive old projects. Throw away anything I haven't used for a year. Throw away old clutter. Throw away old useless shelves. Decide where everything 'lives'. Buy additional storage if necessary.
5 Talk to Julia about organization tips and setting up the filing system.	

Notice how Owen has gone into detail. 'Get an online calendar' is too vague, whereas 'find an online calendar with reminder function' is much clearer. Owen has described each task using active verbs: clear out, order, find, throw away, etc. Breaking tasks into small, action-orientated steps removes confusion.

Finally, Owen reordered this list into a time-based sequence. He decided where to start, ordered the rest logically, and finished with non-urgent tasks and repetitive habits. (He also identified a new task: 'setting up the filing system'. People often come up with new ideas at this stage.)

Owen's list looked like this.

Owen's sequenced action plan		
Milestone	**Task**	**Actions**
1 Complete these tasks first	Order shelves and box files for the office.	Make sure I get the right ones (check with Julia). Find out who the health and safety officer is and ask for chair recommendations. Order chair, shelves, box files and laptop stand via Purchasing.
2 When new shelves arrive	Clear out the office.	Sort through old papers, documents, etc, and archive old projects. Throw away anything I haven't used for a year. Throw away old clutter. Throw away old useless shelves. Decide where everything 'lives'. Buy additional storage if necessary.
3 When the office is sorted	a Buy a little notepad for the to-do list.	There are A6 notepads in the stationery cupboard; I'll collect one from there. Keep it with me and remember to use it whenever anything crops up. Get a desk-tidy as well.
	b Talk to Julia about organization tips and setting up the filing system. c Find an online calendar (with reminder function that I can access via my phone)	Add the times for checking voicemails and emails twice a day. Draw up a list of repetitive tasks and add them into the calendar on 'repeat'. Use the calendar to record meeting times, etc. Add a reminder to check my to-do list each morning. Add a reminder to tidy my desk each evening.
4 Habits I'll need to get into	a Checking voicemails and emails b Adding meetings into my calendar c Checking my to-do list each morning d Tidying my desk each evening e Using my filing system!	

Owen now has a comprehensive action plan. Notice how his tasks are grouped into 'milestones': deciding where to start, what comes next, what comes after that, and so on. This will help him stay organized and on track. If he undertakes each task, repeatedly where necessary, he will accomplish his goal. All that remains is deciding when to start.

Owen's progress

To begin with, Owen made excellent progress. He ordered equipment, reorganized his office, and even repainted. New shelves were assembled and documents filed away. In fact, everything was running smoothly – until he noticed an ugly pile of documents on his desk. Owen realized that something had gone wrong.

His plan included the habit 'using my filing system' – but this was far too vague. Julia, his helpful colleague, advised him to take the following steps:

1 Each evening, gather up all 'unplaced' paperwork.

2 Go through it, placing appropriate documents in your in-tray (or your pending tray) if applicable.

3 Place remaining documents in the appropriate box file.

4 Empty your out-tray and place each document in the appropriate box file.

Owen found this advice helpful because it was specific. He gratefully updated his action plan.

Like Owen, whenever things go wrong, ask yourself: 'Do I know what to do next?' Identifying your next step(s) often dispels the fog of confusion.

Now it's your turn. Drawing up your action plan is a fundamental step. You need to know where to start and what to do next. Let's go through the planning process now.

Action plans are best kept to a maximum of six months in length. Keep this in mind when setting long-term goals. You can always create subsequent plans later.

⏰ *Exercise 12*

DRAWING UP YOUR ACTION PLAN

This exercise takes around 30 minutes. It identifies the steps required to achieve your goal. Use it whenever you need to define a goal.

 Start by summarizing your goal in the middle of a blank sheet of A4 paper.

Reread the measurable outcomes associated with your goal. Close your eyes and imagine experiencing them. Ask yourself: 'How can I make this happen?' Scribble down everything you can think of. Refer to Owen's action plan diagram on page 68 if required.

→ **Simple tasks** Achieving goals means ticking boxes. What tasks do you need to complete?

→ **Complex tasks** These are anything that involves multiple steps.

→ **Habits** Some goals require repetitious action. What habits do you need to establish? Are there bad habits you need to stop?

→ **Resources** Do you need help, equipment or space to achieve your goal?

For the next ten minutes, let your pen run free and scribble ideas down quickly. Don't censor your thoughts or put them in any order; you will sort through them later. Mark any habits with an (h) so they stand out. Be comprehensive. Write everything down – no matter how obvious. No job is too small for this brainstorming session.

Spend as long as necessary on this. Take a 15-minute break when you have finished.

Then read through your list with fresh eyes. Are there glaring omissions? If there are, add them.

Next, we'll rewrite these notes into a list format. This step works best on a word processor. Make a table like this:

Task	Actions

→ Ask yourself: 'What must come first?' Pick out the tasks that *must* be completed before everything else. These are the preparatory steps, purchases, research, 'clearing the decks', etc.

→ Starting with the first task(s), rewrite your notes into a list format. Keep asking yourself: 'And what comes next?'

→ Then, break these tasks into smaller steps if required. Consider each of the actions you'll need to carry out in order to make progress.

→ Organize the tasks into milestones, as Owen did previously. Sorting your tasks into sequential milestones builds focus and desire.

→ Next, expand the description of each task using specific action-orientated language, e.g. 'Unpack the boxes', rather than 'Sort boxes'. Make your plan clear and easy to follow.

You should now have a comprehensive list of specific, clearly described tasks, ordered into a logical, time-based sequence.

Complete the list by adding any habits you need to establish.

How many tasks are on your list? Did you break them down into smaller steps? Does the order seem about right? You will no doubt amend, expand upon and delete steps as we progress. As with everything, flexibility is key.

→ Problems with action plans

Some action plans may seem highly repetitive. For example, if your goal is to study a language course each night, your plan could look something like this:

Task	Actions
Choose the language course	*Order the course from the Internet.*
Subscribe to the course	*Study Chapter 1.* *Study Chapter 2.* *Study Chapter 3.*

… and so on. Clearly, such a plan is no use. The aim is to go into *detail*. For example:

Task	Actions
Before ordering the language course	*Declutter my study area.*
Choose the language course	*Pay for the course.*
Subscribe to the course	*Spend 30 minutes figuring out the syllabus.* *Update this action plan with tasks from the syllabus.*
Start learning the language	*Learn the first 10 basic words.* *Practise writing for 30 minutes.* *Practise speaking for 30 minutes.*

This plan is much more meaningful. In another example, rather than writing 'Go to the gym', describe the exercises in detail. Your action plan should be as clear as possible. Aim to update it as you progress.

Summary

Motivation cannot exist without a motive, and you will benefit from this thorough approach to goal setting. Just committing to your goal in writing has set you apart, so take a moment to acknowledge that fact.

If you have not yet completed the goal-setting exercises, it is not too late to start! Refresh your understanding of consequences (see Chapter 2) and take it from there. Waiting for the right time, or for somebody to do this for you, will only lead to disappointment. Take small steps, and finish what you started.

In coming chapters you will be encouraged to work on your goal. Should you complete it while we are still progressing through our work together, reread Chapters 4 and 5 and set yourself a new goal. Defining your goals thoroughly gives you the best chance of success.

What I have learned

→ What are my thoughts, feelings and insights on what I have read so far?

_____

_____

_____

_____

Use the space below to summarize any actions you identify as a result of reading this chapter.

_____

_____

_____

_____

_____

Where to next?

You now have a framework for making your compelling vision a reality. Execute your action plan, repeatedly where required, and your success is virtually guaranteed. It *is* that simple.

There will be challenges to overcome and adjustments to make. Life's surprises often seem to conspire against us. It is important to make full use of your resources so, with that in mind, let's return our attention to the question of time.

6 *Identifying your 'goal time'*

In this chapter:
- ▶ you will learn how to schedule time effectively
- ▶ you will discover the four simple rules for valuing your time
- ▶ you will create your 'goal timetable' by mapping out your 'goal time'.

In previous chapters, you thoroughly defined a goal to work on. It now has substance, structure and sequence; it is becoming real. We now need to integrate this goal into your life, which means marrying it to your time.

Before we continue, have you:

- ▶ written your compelling vision statement?
- ▶ filled out a SMART goal statement?
- ▶ compiled your action plan?

It is not too late to complete these steps! Thoroughly defining your goals – no matter how simple they are – is vital to sustained motivation. Before continuing, ensure that you are on top of things. Otherwise you risk losing your way.

> *'May you live all the days of your life.'*
>
> Jonathan Swift

→ Simple scheduling

Achieving your goal will take time, so you need to know *when* to act. Without this clarity, you're likely to drift. There would be no urgency or purpose.

Some goals (usually work-based) are married to the main portion of our day. Other goals require us to use our 'spare' time – working in addition to our daily responsibilities. Each scenario brings its own challenges.

When goals are *supposed* to take up most of our time, we can grow complacent or distracted. Alternatively, we might feel intimidated by the amount of work ahead of us. Either way, we busy ourselves with less important matters. Using our spare time also presents challenges. We might feel pressured by lack of time, or resent using it for 'work' (not unfairly: rest and play cannot wisely be neglected). Tiredness becomes an issue, and motivation is difficult without energy.

Either way, making the most of your time is crucial. There are several approaches to this – some simple and some complex. We'll keep it simple.

Exercise 13

MAPPING YOUR TIME

This exercise takes about ten minutes. It identifies your ideal times for getting things done. Use it whenever you need an overview of your available time.

The exercise refers to going to 'work', which could mean any of a range of activities including employment, school, college, university, volunteering, caring or working from home.

 The following table shows seven columns, labelled Monday through to Sunday, with the time of key events during a person's typical working day. It has been filled in with everything that *has* to happen. Use this example to guide you when you fill in your own blank table, shown on page 81. Use your timetable to see the gaps, the available chunks of time when you could work on your goal.

Weekly timetable

Key events	Monday	Tuesday	Wednesday	Thursday	Friday	Saturday	Sunday
Wake/get up	7.30	7.30	7.30	7.30	7.30	10ish	10ish
	Breakfast, shower, etc.	Breakfast, shower, etc.	Breakfast, shower, etc.	Breakfast, shower, etc.	Breakfast, shower, etc.	Breakfast, shower, etc.	Breakfast, shower, etc.
Set off for work (or wherever)	8.15	8.15	8.15	8.15	8.15		
	Commute to work	Commute to work	Commute to work	Commute to work	Commute to work		
Arrive at work	8.45	8.45	8.45	8.45	8.45		
	Emails, phone calls, etc.	Emails, phone calls, etc.	Emails, phone calls, etc.	Emails, phone calls, etc.	Emails, phone calls, etc.	11–2 Take Richard to his football match	11–6 Spend time with family, lunch, chores, etc.
Morning break	10–10.15	10–10.15	10–10.15	10–10.15	10–.10.15		
	General work	General work	General work	General work	General work		
Lunch	12	12	12	12	12		
	Lunch break	Lunch break	Lunch break	Lunch break	Lunch break		
Restart work	12.45	12.45	12.45	12.45	12.45		
	General work	1–2 Department meeting 2–6 General work	General work 3–6 Weekly staff reports	General work	General work	2–6 Errands, lunch, etc.	
Leave work	6	6	6	6	6		
	Commute home	Commute home	Football	Commute home	Commute home		
Arrive home	6.30	6.30	8	6.30	6.30		
	Change, eat, spend time with kids	Change, eat, spend time with kids	Say goodnight to kids, eat.	Change, eat, spend time with kids	Change, eat, spend time with kids	6–10 Eat, spend time with family	6–8 Eat, spend time with family
Settle down for evening	8.30	8.30	9.30	8.30	8.30		
	Relax	Relax	Relax	Relax	Relax DVD night	10–12 Relax	8–11 Relax
Go to bed	11	11	11	11	12	12	11
Other commitments in day		Department meeting	Weekly staff reports Football				

Will you work on your goal during the day? In this example, it might be possible to make time as follows:

→ Monday: 10 a.m.–12 p.m.; 12.45 p.m.–6 p.m.

→ Tuesday: 10 a.m.–12 p.m.; 2 p.m.–6 p.m.

→ Wednesday: 10 a.m.–12 p.m.; 12.45 p.m.–3 p.m.

Does your goal require you to use your spare time? In this example, it might be possible to make time during the following periods:

→ Monday: 8.30 p.m.–11 p.m.

→ Saturday: 2 p.m.–5 p.m.

→ Sunday: 11 a.m.–6 p.m.; 8 p.m.–10 p.m.

These are your chunks of 'goal time'. Is your time plentiful or scarce? Either way, the aim is to carry out your action plan during this time. This is how goals are achieved.

For each key moment, 'block out' the time taken by what follows:

→ From waking up, the time it takes to get out of bed, eat breakfast, shower, dress, etc.

→ From the time you set off for work (or wherever), the time taken up by commuting.

→ Any time spent on repetitive morning commitments, e.g. team meetings, replying to emails, the 'Wednesday reports', lectures, etc.

→ The time taken by your lunch break.

→ Any time spent on repetitive afternoon commitments.

→ From the time you leave work, the evening commute.

→ The time it takes to change, shower, eat, spend some time with the kids, and so on...

Weekly timetable							
Key events	Monday	Tuesday	Wednesday	Thursday	Friday	Saturday	Sunday
Wake/get up							
Set off for work (or wherever)							
Arrive at work							
Morning break							
Lunch							
Restart work							
Afternoon break							
Leave work							
Arrive home							
Settle down for evening							
Go to bed							
Other commitments in day							

The aim is to build a representative idea of your typical working week.

Next, identify the non-essential events that happen each day:

→ Note the time you start relaxing in the evening and block out the time taken.

→ Identify time spent regularly on hobbies, interests, socializing and visiting relatives, and block out that time.

It is okay to generalize. If you're out one evening per week, albeit on different days, block out *just one evening* to be representative.

Spend no more than five to ten minutes on this. Be comprehensive without going into forensic detail. You will tighten it up as you go along.

If you work shifts or unusual hours, complete this process for each shift pattern. The aim is the same: to create a typical overview of your working week(s).

Finally, carry out the same steps for the weekend (or your regular days off). Start with your usual rising time and block out the tasks, errands and activities typically carried out.

→ Optimizing your time

How much time do you waste? *Honestly* review your typical week. For instance, do you waste much time at work? People often do; it's an easy trap to fall into.

Time outside work can be very limited. We generally have a little spare time in the morning, perhaps some time at lunch, and a reasonable amount during the evening. There may be time available at the weekend, depending on other commitments.

In Chapter 2 you completed Exercise 3: 'How much time do you really have?' People often feel shocked by the results. Your weekly timetable can be equally disheartening: so much time is given over to other responsibilities. Perhaps you now understand how precious time really is.

Is it possible to optimize the time you do have? Ask yourself questions like:

▶ Where is the wastage?

▶ Can I get up earlier?

▶ Can I run errands during my lunch break rather than at weekends?

▶ Do I really need to spend so much time answering emails each morning?

▶ Can I sacrifice a leisure activity to spend more time on my goal?

▶ Do I waste time dithering or dawdling? (Hint: we all do!)

▶ Are my mornings/afternoons/evenings/weekends spent cheaply?

If there are adjustments you can *easily* make, go ahead and amend the time(s) identified previously. However, be realistic: optimizing your time is not easy. Take small steps or you will become overwhelmed.

Difficult transitions

People often struggle to switch between different types of work. It is hard to study after working all day. Similarly, if you work 'in your business' during the morning, working 'on your business' later feels challenging. The change of pace distracts us.

Combat this by creating firm boundaries. Allow yourself time to refresh yourself and relax; even 30 minutes would do. It is just as important not to skimp on rest and play. Neglecting your basic needs weakens motivation, so a sensible amount of playtime and rest is vital in all but the most pressing circumstances.

→ How to value your time

We rush to avoid being late for work, but we treat our *own* time with far less urgency. This must change if you're hoping to achieve your goals.

Valuing your time means following these four simple rules:

1 Start when you're supposed to start.

2 Divide your time into 'action blocks' where necessary.

3 Work on your goal without distraction.

4 Take regular breaks promptly.

Changing your relationship with time overnight is impossible. However, learning certain skills will improve your approach. All it takes is practice. Let's explore the rationale behind each rule.

START WHEN YOU'RE SUPPOSED TO START

People start work on time because lateness is penalized. However, running late for your own life is far worse. It causes anxiety, frustration, unfulfilled potential, depression ... and deep future regret. This is far worse than any 'written warning'.

Valuing your time means starting on time. If you've decided to work on your goal at 7.30 p.m., it makes little sense to start something else at 7.25 p.m.

DIVIDE YOUR TIME INTO 'ACTION BLOCKS'

Since time is fluid and difficult to track, with one moment running into the next, it is beneficial, when working on your goal for 90 minutes or more, to break your time into 'action blocks'. The benefits include the following:

▶ You have a target to aim for, which combats complacency.

▶ Smaller blocks are less overwhelming and so you'll feel less discouraged.

▶ Regular breaks maintain concentration. Our brains need to rest and cool down!

Breaking time into 'action blocks' takes willingness and practice. There are several strategies you could try:

1 **Break time into 90-minute chunks, taking a 30-minute rest after each one.** Many accomplished violinists practise in 90-minute blocks. You might have to build up to that level of motivation – but it is possible.

2 **Break time into 45-minute chunks with a 15-minute rest period.** It seems logical to break time into hourly units; this workbook refers to 45-minute chunks (with 15-minute breaks).

3 **Break time into 25-minute chunks with a 5-minute rest period.** This approach is sometimes known as the Pomodoro Technique®. The same principles apply. Some find these smaller blocks too 'stop-and-start', but they are worth a try if you're struggling with longer chunks. You can increase the length of each block as your motivation increases.

Dividing time into blocks allows us to set targets. For example, an eight-hour stretch becomes seven 45-minute action blocks (including a 60-minute break taken midway through). This gives you something concrete to aim for, which strengthens motivation.

Adapt these 'action blocks' to your circumstances. With 90 minutes of free time each evening, try 3 × 25-minute blocks (incorporating 5-minute breaks), or 2 × 40-minute blocks (with a 10-minute break). Try to stay within the 25- to 45-minute range, and keep things as consistent as possible.

Only use action blocks if necessary

Breaking time into action blocks is not always necessary. For example, some goals require us to accomplish small, repetitive tasks. Although this workbook focuses on working for *stretches of time*, you can adapt these techniques as required.

Some goals might not fit 45-minute 'action blocks' (e.g. spending an hour in the gym or 30 minutes cooking), so be flexible – the techniques in this chapter are presented as guidelines.

WORK ON YOUR GOAL WITHOUT DISTRACTION

All your efforts so far will count for nothing if you don't actually work on your goal! This means making a start, staying focused, and persisting until your next break. It *doesn't* mean any of the following:

- ▶ Checking Facebook, Twitter, Tumblr, LinkedIn, Pinterest, Tagged or Instagram
- ▶ Checking and replying to texts
- ▶ Checking and replying to emails
- ▶ Checking the latest football/fashion/science/philately blogs
- ▶ Watching funny cat videos on YouTube
- ▶ Drinking endless cups of tea or coffee
- ▶ Smoking
- ▶ Eating
- ▶ Watching your favourite box set
- ▶ Daydreaming about how fantastic it will be when you've completed your goal
- ▶ Receiving calls from friends
- ▶ Going out
- ▶ Playing Football Manager
- ▶ Indulging in a spot of retail therapy
- ▶ Worrying about not achieving your goal.

Your mind would *love* to draw you into such activities, as they create a false sense of reward while reducing the stress associated with challenging yourself. Low motivation is a compelling trap built from our distorted perceptions. Use your 'goal time' to work on your goal – and nothing else. Although this may seem obvious, we often forget to do this.

TAKE REGULAR BREAKS

Regular breaks are vital, especially when you are working for 90 minutes or more. A true break involves leaving your work area and focusing on something else. If you're working on a computer, focus your eyes elsewhere. Unless you allow your mind and body to rest, it is not really a break.

Using your time wisely means you *deserve* a small break, for several good reasons:

▶ Without breaks, time is no longer divided into blocks. The old problems then arise.

▶ Studies show that regular breaks enhance effort and concentration. Your performance will slacken without them.

When dividing your time into action blocks, take a prompt break after each one. After four hours or so, take a longer rest (30–45 minutes). This is especially important when you have been working for eight hours or more.

Valuing your time is paramount but it does require *control*. Following these four simple rules changes everything: with practice, you could double your achievements in life. Think about that for a moment.

→ Marrying your goal to your time

Previously, you created your action plan – the tasks required to achieve your goal. And now that you have identified your available 'goal time', here are the next steps to take:

1 Determine the best time to work towards your goal.

2 When the time comes, carry out your action plan – following the four simple rules above.

3 Keep going until you have achieved your goal.

These steps may seem too easy, but all success is arrived at in this way. There will be obstacles to overcome and adjustments to make, even with solid motivation. However, following these steps means you will succeed – eventually.

Let's look at an example goal, mapped across time:

Goal: I am becoming a self-employed nutrition therapist, with a steady client base, a popular blog and a weekly guest slot on local radio.	
How am I doing this?	When am I doing this?
Working on the copy for my website	8.30 p.m.–10.30 p.m. Monday, Tuesday, Thursday
Researching available office space on the Internet	Lunch break at work, Monday to Friday
Emailing everyone from my nutrition course	8.30 p.m.–9 p.m. Friday
Researching local networking groups	9 p.m.–10.30 p.m. Friday
Finding practice insurance	1 p.m.–2 p.m. Saturday
Finishing copy for website if needed	2 p.m.–5 p.m. Saturday

This goal involves filling blocks of time with various tasks. Completing these tasks at the designated times will achieve the goal. Time and action are married together.

→ Scheduling small, repetitive tasks

Some goals may require you to carry out small, repetitive tasks. Here is an example:

Goal: I am learning how to cook the following meals: chicken curry, spaghetti bolognese, chilli con carne, black olive risotto, and steak and chips.	
Timing	Task
8 a.m. (Tuesday, Wednesday, Friday)	Check available ingredients, and decide which recipe to prepare accordingly
8 a.m. (Monday and Thursday)	Check ingredients and draw up shopping list
6 p.m. (Monday and Thursday)	Go to the supermarket and buy ingredients
7 p.m.–8 p.m. (Monday to Friday)	Prepare (and eat!) evening meal
5 p.m.– 6 p.m. (Sunday)	Prepare evening meal

This goal involves regularly checking ingredients and compiling shopping lists. Obviously, this wouldn't take 45 minutes! Carry out small tasks when required, and complete action blocks as necessary. For example:

▶ **getting fit:** taking supplements in the morning (habit); keeping a food diary (habit); going to the gym in the evening (action block)

▶ **becoming organized at work:** working diligently during the day (action blocks) and tidying my desk each night (habit)

▶ **completing a correspondence course:** check the online forums daily for ten minutes (habit) and spend several hours each weekend completing course materials (action blocks).

Your goal might involve establishing habits at certain times, filling blocks of time with activity, or a combination of the two. Either way, take action when required and you will succeed. All it takes is consistency.

Let's finalize the best times to work towards your goal. You will then know when to execute your action plan and achieve your goal.

 *Exercise 14*

CREATING A 'GOAL TIMETABLE'

This exercise takes five to ten minutes. It identifies your 'goal time' – the time for taking action. Use this exercise when deciding when to work on your goal.

Earlier in this chapter, you identified your spare time by completing Exercise 13, 'Mapping your time'. Review your timetable now, and identify the time you could work on your goal. Be realistic – avoid filling every spare moment. Accept the need for rest and play.

 Now write out your designated goal time, as in this example.

Goal time:

    Monday: 7.30–8.30 a.m.; 8–10 p.m.

    Tuesday: 7.30–8.30 a.m.; 8–10 p.m.

    Wednesday: 7.30–8.30 a.m.

    Thursday: None

    Friday: 7.30–8.30 a.m.; 8–10 p.m.

Saturday: 10 a.m.–6 p.m.

Sunday: 10 a.m.–4 p.m.

Then, if appropriate, break your time into 'action blocks'. This example uses 45-minute blocks with a 15-minute break, with a longer break where necessary.

Goal time:

Monday: 7.30–8.30 a.m. (45×1); 8–10 p.m. (45×2)

Tuesday: 7.30–8.30 a.m. (45×1); 8–10 p.m. (45×2)

Wednesday: 7.30–8.30 a.m. (45×1)

Thursday: None

Friday: 7.30–8.30 a.m. (45×1); 8–10 p.m. (45×2)

Saturday: 10 a.m.–6 p.m. (45×7)

Sunday: 10 a.m.–4 p.m. (45×5)

Note how the free hour each morning has been turned into a 45-minute block. The alternative is working for the whole hour, which would be fine. Saturday's schedule includes a 45-minute break, taken from 2–2.45 p.m., meaning that the finish time would actually be 5.45 p.m.

Review your identified times, and check that you're not overcommitting yourself. If you're not a morning person, be realistic! Identify times you're likely to use effectively.

Does your goal involve carrying out quick tasks at certain points? If so, schedule them into your timetable, if appropriate, like this:

Goal time:

Monday: 7.30–8.30 a.m. (45×1); 8–10 p.m. (45×2)

Tuesday: 7.30–8.30 a.m. (45×1); 8–10 p.m. (45×2)

Wednesday: 7.30–8.30 a.m. (45×1)

Thursday: None

Friday: 7.30–8.30 a.m. (45×1); 8–10 p.m. (45×2)

Saturday: 10 a.m.–6 p.m. (45×7)

Sunday: 10 a.m.–4 p.m. (45×5)

8.15 a.m. (Monday to Friday) – check emails

8 p.m. (Monday to Friday) – return voicemails

This timetable involves completing a couple of quick tasks at certain times. Avoid overburdening yourself with such tasks. Ideally, set no more than three per day.

Print out your timetable and keep it visible, ideally where you will work on your goal. Add these times to your online or smartphone calendar; the more reminders you get, the better.

You should now have a clear overview of your 'goal time'. If you use these times to execute your action plan, following the four simple rules for valuing your time, you will make good progress.

Flexibility is key

This process might seem complicated at first, but it really is simple. Identify your available time and value it. Schedule tasks into that time, dividing it into blocks if necessary, and you will make progress.

Making any plan work means being flexible. Inevitably, unforeseen circumstances will curtail your available time (and sometimes you'll gain additional time to use). Be flexible and adapt to your circumstances – make the most of what you have.

Summary

So far, you have created several documents: your compelling vision statement, your SMART goal definition, your action plan, and now your goal timetable. This means:

1 You know what you want to do.

2 You know why you want to do it.

3 You know what steps to take.

4 You know when to take those steps.

We have spent a significant amount of time creating these documents. This thoroughness will pay off. Motivation is impossible without clarity.

What I have learned

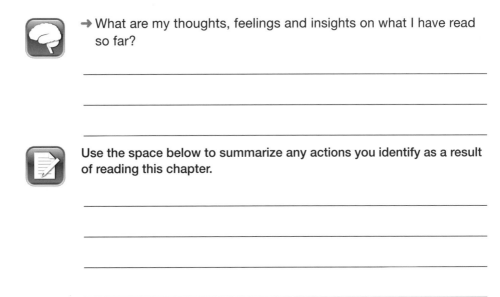

→ What are my thoughts, feelings and insights on what I have read so far?

_____

_____

_____

Use the space below to summarize any actions you identify as a result of reading this chapter.

_____

_____

_____

_____

Where to next?

Next, let's focus on the skills required to build motivation. Before continuing, ensure that you have completed all the exercises in Chapters 3 to 6. They don't take long, and it's never too late to start!

7 Demotivating challenges

In this chapter:

▶ you will explore 'demotivating challenges' – and how they rob you of your time

▶ you will learn about the BET model and how it helps build motivation

▶ you will identify the challenges you face and begin the process of overcoming them.

If people were governed solely by logic, motivation would never be a problem. We'd work contentedly on our goals and rarely succumb to distraction. Unfortunately, motivation is more complicated than that.

Our thoughts, beliefs, habits and emotions often hold us back. These moments, sometimes referred to as 'demotivating challenges', are created by unhelpful signals in the brain. Demotivating challenges feel real and compelling, but they are extremely destructive.

'*We cannot change anything unless we accept it.*'

Carl Jung

→ Identifying demotivating challenges

Previously we met Matt, the talented young boxer who dreams of becoming a champion. Despite life's many temptations, he never skips training. His emotional mind has decided: *choose hard work now and enjoy your future*. There is simply no conflict. As a result, Matt overcomes demotivated moments with ease. He rises to the challenge because he wants to achieve his dream. With practice, you can also learn this skill. Demotivated behaviour will become a thing of the past.

THE ANATOMY OF DEMOTIVATION

Demotivating challenges reflect our thoughts, feelings, habits and behaviours.

Do you recognize *thoughts* such as these?

- ▶ 'I've not got time to do this now.'
- ▶ 'It's too difficult. I give up!'
- ▶ 'I'll just do this other thing first.'

Perhaps you can recognize these *emotions*:

- ▶ feeling reluctant to work on your goal
- ▶ feeling tempted to do something more interesting
- ▶ feeling too despondent and giving up.

Our *habits* frequently demotivate us:

- ▶ switching away from our work – without even realizing
- ▶ missing appointments or tasks because we 'forgot'
- ▶ habitually refusing to act while on 'autopilot'.

Demotivating challenges are most obvious in our *behaviour*:

- ▶ unnecessarily over-preparing rather than starting
- ▶ taking lots of little breaks instead of settling down to work
- ▶ endlessly daydreaming about a better future.

These challenges are caused by our *state of mind* at that time. Our thoughts, feelings, habits and behaviours influence each other, as in these examples.

- ▶ **Thoughts affect emotions and behaviours.** Demotivated thoughts lead to demotivated feelings and behaviours. This is obvious perhaps, but we often forget to guard against it.
- ▶ **Emotions change thoughts and behaviours.** Feel *reluctant* to act, and you might excuse yourself from taking action. Demotivated behaviour becomes more likely.
- ▶ **Behaviours change thoughts and feelings.** Surfing the Internet, instead of writing your essay, will affect your thoughts and feelings. Motivation weakens even further.

Even worse, demotivated thoughts, feelings and behaviours, when repeated over time, turn into nasty habits. To change this, we must first increase our awareness.

→ The problem of low awareness

Demotivated behaviour is sometimes easy to spot. However, it's not always straightforward. Our thoughts, feelings and even our actions can pass us by. Have you ever felt stuck in a demotivated state? It's like falling into a trance; nothing is more destructive than the vortex of compulsive avoidance.

Are you always aware when your motivation falters? Can you identify the thoughts, emotions, behaviours and habits that demotivate you? We need to gather this information, and using the BET model described below will help.

THE BET MODEL

The BET model is a simple tool for recording behaviour, emotions, thoughts and habits. It uses a quick questionnaire to identify demotivating challenges as they arise. This means paying extra attention at various points:

1 Before starting work on your goal

2 While working on your goal

3 When taking breaks

4 When returning from breaks.

You might become demotivated through bad habits, demotivating thoughts or feelings, or distracting behaviours. This tool records those moments and reveals vital clues. With better awareness, you can then overcome these challenges.

To see this in action, let's review another case study.

Rhodri's story

Rhodri knew he was drifting through life. Now approaching 30, and having held the same job for a decade, he was desperate for a new challenge. He had tried to change jobs in the past, but he always seemed to lose focus. Life had just become too comfortable.

Rhodri set himself a goal, created an action plan and identified his 'goal time'. As for most people, this meant evenings and weekends. Then, to gauge his progress, Rhodri was shown the BET model. This meant making simple notes on a series of record sheets whenever he felt demotivated. The aim was to help him understand the *nature* of his demotivated moments.

Day 1 of the BET model

Rhodri was asked to carry out his action plan in the allotted time, ideally following the rules from Chapter 6:

1 Start when you're supposed to start.

2 Divide your time into 'action blocks' where necessary.

3 Work on your goal without distraction.

4 Take regular breaks promptly.

He was given a form (known as a BET record) to make notes. He had it to hand *before* starting.

BET record

Date:

Task:

Part 1: starting on time

Behaviour:
Emotions:
Thoughts:
Habit (Y/N):

Part 2: working on my goal

During: 1	2	3
Behaviour:		
Emotions:		
Thoughts:		
Habit (Y/N):		

During: 4	5	6
Behaviour:		
Emotions:		
Thoughts:		
Habit (Y/N):		

Part 3: taking prompt breaks

Start of break:	**End of break:**
Behaviour:	Behaviour:
Emotions:	Emotions:
Thoughts:	Thoughts:
Habit (Y/N):	Habit (Y/N):

When the time came, Rhodri attempted his first 45-minute action block. However, it soon became obvious that he had started late. Rhodri recorded the experience by answering the following questions.

BET questionnaire

1 What *behaviour* did you do instead of working on your goal?

2 What *emotions* did you feel about working on your goal?

3 What *thoughts* discouraged you? Did you excuse yourself from taking action? Did you think negatively about the task ahead?

4 Was any of this *habitual*? (Did you distract yourself without consciously deciding to do so?)

Here are his answers.

BET record

Date: *15 January*

Task: *Rewriting my CV*

Part 1: starting on time

Behaviour: *Twitter, Facebook*
Emotions: *Complacent*
Thoughts: *I'll do it in a bit*
Habit (Y/N): *It felt automatic*

Part 2: working on my goal

During: 1	During: 2	During: 3
Behaviour:		
Emotions:		
Thoughts:		
Habit (Y/N):		

During: 4	During: 5	During: 6
Behaviour:		
Emotions:		
Thoughts:		
Habit (Y/N):		

Part 3: taking prompt breaks

Start of break:	End of break:
Behaviour:	Behaviour:
Emotions:	Emotions:
Thoughts:	Thoughts:
Habit (Y/N):	Habit (Y/N):

Had Rhodri started on time, he could have skipped this first set of questions. Instead, he wrote down his answers before carrying on. Notice how his answers are brief. These questions should take just moments to answer.

Rhodri then started working on his goal. He decided to work in 45-minute action blocks. During this time Rhodri was asked to note any distractions, using the six columns on the same record sheet. There were several distractions over the next action block. After 45 minutes, his BET record now looked like this:

BET record

Date: *15 January*
Task: *Rewriting my CV*

Part 1: starting on time

Behaviour: *Twitter, Facebook*
Emotions: Complacent
Thoughts: I'll do it in a bit
Habit (Y/N): *It felt automatic*

Part 2: working on my goal

During:	1	2	3
Behaviour:	*Twitter (20 mins)*	*Went on Twitter (5 mins)*	*Checked email (7 mins)*
Emotions:	*Frustrated; bored*	*Bored.*	*Tempted*
Thoughts:	*I hate doing this*	*N/A*	*I've got an email*
Habit (Y/N):	*No.*	*I think so*	*No*

During:	4	5	6
Behaviour:	*Twitter (10 mins)*		
Emotions:	*N/A*		
Thoughts:	*N/A*		
Habit (Y/N):	*Definitely!*		

Part 3: taking prompt breaks

Start of break:	End of break:
Behaviour:	Behaviour:
Emotions:	Emotions:
Thoughts:	Thoughts:
Habit (Y/N):	Habit (Y/N):

Rhodri didn't do too well on this first day, becoming demotivated for a combined total of 42 minutes (out of a 45-minute block)! He did not make it to Part 3 of the questionnaire. Feeling quite despondent, he resolved to try again the next day.

Notice Rhodri's last period of distraction: ten minutes spent on Twitter. He identified this as a bad habit because it was automatic and thoughtless. This exercise identifies the *nature* of our demotivated moments, which will prove important later.

Day 2 of the BET model

The next day, Rhodri reattempted his task and managed to start on time. Let's pick up with Rhodri after the first 45 minutes.

BET record

Date: *16 January*
Task: *Rewriting my CV*

Part 1: starting on time

Behaviour:
Emotions:
Thoughts:
Habit (Y/N):

Part 2: working on my goal

During:	1	2	3
Behaviour:	*Twitter (4 mins)*	*Twitter (2 mins)*	*Email (4 mins)*
Emotions:	*Frustrated*	*Frustrated*	*N/A*
Thoughts:	*It's okay to go on it*	*N/A*	*N/A*
Habit (Y/N):			

During:	4	5	6
Behaviour:			
Emotions:			
Thoughts:			
Habit (Y/N):			

Part 3: taking prompt breaks

Start of break:	**End of break:**
Behaviour:	Behaviour:
Emotions:	Emotions:
Thoughts:	Thoughts:
Habit (Y/N):	Habit (Y/N):

We can see that Rhodri has made some progress. He skipped Part 1 of the questionnaire because he started on time. He did succumb to periods of distraction, albeit only briefly. (As a rule, only record losses of motivation lasting 60 seconds or longer.)

Having completed 45 minutes relatively unscathed, Rhodri took his break and returned. Unfortunately, he found himself running late. He completed the questionnaire once more. Here are his answers.

BET record

Date: *16 January*
Task: *Rewriting my CV*

Part 1: starting on time

Behaviour:
Emotions:
Thoughts:
Habit (Y/N):

Part 2: working on my goal

During:	1	2	3
Behaviour:	*Twitter (4 mins)*	*Twitter (2 mins)*	*Email (4 mins)*
Emotions:	*Frustrated*	*Frustrated*	*N/A*
Thoughts:	*It's okay to go on it*	*N/A*	*N/A*
Habit (Y/N):			

During:	4	5	6
Behaviour:			
Emotions:			
Thoughts:			
Habit (Y/N):			

Part 3: taking prompt breaks

Start of break:	**End of break:**
Behaviour: *Twitter (44 mins)*	Behaviour:
Emotions: *N/A*	Emotions:
Thoughts: *N/A*	Thoughts:
Habit (Y/N): *Definitely*	Habit (Y/N):

It doesn't look good! Instead of taking a break, Rhodri stayed on his laptop and lost himself online. Taking proper breaks means walking away and focusing elsewhere.

Day 3 of the BET model

Once more, Rhodri worked on his goal. Here are his results.

BET record

Date: *17 January*
Task: *Rewriting my CV*

Part 1: starting on time

Behaviour: *Twitter*
Emotions: *N/A*
Thoughts: *N/A*
Habit (Y/N): *Definitely!*

Part 2: working on my goal

During:	1	2	3
Behaviour:	*Twitter (2 mins)*	*Twitter (2 mins)*	*Sent a text message*
Emotions:	*Frustrated*	*Frustrated*	*Tempted*
Thoughts:	*N/A*	*N/A*	*It's okay, it's just a text*
Habit (Y/N):	*Yes*	*Yes*	*No*

During:	4	5	6
Behaviour:			
Emotions:			
Thoughts:			
Habit (Y/N):			

Part 3: taking prompt breaks

Start of break:	**End of break:**
Behaviour: *Twitter (2 mins)*	Behaviour: *Twitter!!! (4 mins)*
Emotions: *N/A*	Emotions: *Tempted*
Thoughts: *N/A*	Thoughts: *I'll start in a bit*
Habit (Y/N): *Definitely*	Habit (Y/N): *Perhaps; semi-habit*

There has been further improvement. Although Rhodri started late, his demotivated periods were brief and he managed his break quite well. His main problem seems to be with Twitter: it looks like a mindless bad habit. He would clearly benefit by logging out of the site after each session. This would break the the habit and dramatically improve his focus.

In summary

This approach sheds invaluable light on the challenges we face. Notice how Rhodri struggles when frustration takes over. His attention shifts elsewhere and motivation is lost. He now knows to be vigilant at such times.

Now it is your turn. We'll begin by identifying your next 'goal time'. When the time comes, use the BET model to examine any demotivated moments. We can then start to change your responses to those challenges. Increasing your awareness is key.

PUTTING THIS TOGETHER

 In the previous chapter you identified the times you will work on your goal (your 'goal time'). Write down the next ten periods available to you. Leave the 'Number of blocks' field blank if not applicable.

Goal calendar (preview)			
1 Date & time		Number of blocks	
2 Date & time		Number of blocks	
3 Date & time		Number of blocks	
4 Date & time		Number of blocks	
5 Date & time		Number of blocks	
6 Date & time		Number of blocks	
7 Date & time		Number of blocks	
8 Date & time		Number of blocks	
9 Date & time		Number of blocks	
10 Date & time		Number of blocks	

Using your smartphone or online calendar, set an *audible* alarm for each of these times. (Please do not skip this step! This advice is repeated in every chapter.)

 Other types of goal

This workbook describes how to sustain motivation for periods of time because people find that the most challenging. If your goal involves making motivated decisions or carrying out small tasks, the process is the same: follow steps 1–3 below and make notes when you falter.

→ How to take action

Here's the basic plan. Read through the following exercise and familiarize yourself with the steps. It comes in three parts:

▶ **Part 1** describes how to start working on your goal.

▶ **Part 2** describes how to continue working on your goal.

▶ **Part 3** describes how to take – and return from – your breaks.

At any stage, should things things go wrong, make notes about your experiences using the BET questionnaire below.

Our aim is to follow the four simple rules of valuing time:

1 Start when you're supposed to start.

2 Divide your time into 'action blocks' where necessary.

3 Work on your goal without distraction.

4 Take regular breaks promptly.

Recognize the moments where you struggle to motivate yourself as demotivating challenges. Make notes on the experience, following the instructions below.

Exercise 15

WORKING ON YOUR GOAL

This exercise takes 45 minutes (plus stoppages) each time. It encourages you to work on your goal and record any demotivated periods. Complete this exercise every time you attempt an 'action block'.

Part 1: starting on time

Try to start promptly; be where you need to be and have everything you need. Write the date and time, and the task you're working on next, on a new BET record (see below).

If you started late, consider the thoughts, feelings, habits and behaviour that stood in your way. Answer the questionnaire below, using Part 1 of your current BET record.

Then set a 45-minute timer and get off to a good start by taking about two minutes to complete the following steps:

→ Read your compelling vision statement (see Chapter 4).

→ Read your SMART goal statement (see Chapter 5).

→ Read your action plan: which task(s) should you work on next?

Part 2: working on my goal

Now start working on your goal – without distraction – for the remainder of your action block. If your resolve weakens, recognize the experience as a demotivating challenge and try to ease past it.

Each time you lose motivation for more than 60 seconds, use Part 2 of your current BET record to make notes – again, use the questionnaire. Then refocus on your goal.

Part 3: taking prompt breaks

After 45 minutes, start a 15-minute timer and take your break immediately. Leave your work area and focus on something else for a spell. Let your mind cool down!

→ Return from your break after 15 minutes and be ready to start your next action block if scheduled.

→ Again, recognize the temptation to skip breaks (or return from them late) as demotivating challenges; try to ease past them. If you become demotivated around your breaks, complete Part 3 of your BET record using the questionnaire.

If you intend to carry on working, start a new 45-minute timer and follow the steps above. Use a new BET record each time; this information will prove really useful.

It might seem long-winded at first, but it's really very simple. Refer to Rhodri's example if you get stuck. Follow the steps carefully, answer the questionnaire as required, and use a new BET record each time.

If you can start a 45-minute block now, then do so. Otherwise, come back to this page when your next 'goal time' starts. Here's the questionnaire to use if you grind to a halt.

BET questionnaire
1	What **behaviour** did you do instead of working on your goal?
2	What **emotions** did you feel about working on your goal?
3	What **thoughts** discouraged you? Did you excuse yourself from taking action? Did you think negatively about the task ahead?
4	Was any of this **habitual?** (Did you distract yourself without consciously deciding to do so?)

Use this form to record your answers to the BET questions. Here is a blank one to photocopy, or to copy by hand into a page of your notebook.

<u>BET record</u>

Date:

Task:

Part 1: starting on time

Behaviour:
Emotions:
Thoughts:
Habit (Y/N):

Part 2: working on my goal

During:	1	2	3
Behaviour:			
Emotions:			
Thoughts:			
Habit (Y/N):			

During:	4	5	6
Behaviour:			
Emotions:			
Thoughts:			
Habit (Y/N):			

Part 3: taking prompt breaks

Start of break:	**End of break:**
Behaviour:	Behaviour:
Emotions:	Emotions:
Thoughts:	Thoughts:
Habit (Y/N):	Habit (Y/N):

Keep your notes brief while identifying the thoughts, feelings, habits and behaviours behind any demotivated episodes. Tracking your distractions is really important. Our motivation increases simply by holding ourselves accountable.

→ Demotivating challenges

If you feel tempted to avoid working on your goal – or to skip the exercises in this chapter – recognize this experience as a 'demotivating challenge'. Your reluctance is created by unhelpful signals in your brain, and you do not have to give in to them. Instead, make brief notes on the experience. Your insights will prove invaluable.

 Here is a list of the various challenges you may face. Use it when completing your BET records.

Potential challenges		
Demotivating behaviour	**Demotivating emotions**	**Demotivating thoughts**
Any activity other than working towards your goal	**Complacency:** ignoring the importance of working towards your goal, e.g. 'I can't be bothered', or 'It's not important.'	**Plausible excuses:** thoughts that give you permission to focus elsewhere, despite not standing up to scrutiny, e.g. 'I don't have to do this yet', or 'I don't have everything I need.'
Over-planning: excessively planning action instead of taking action	**Reluctance, tiredness, boredom, frustration, anxiety and feeling overwhelmed:** abandoning your commitment to your goal	**Value judgements:** your appraisal of the tasks ahead, e.g. 'It's boring', or 'It's not going to be good enough.'
General dithering: present but not really doing anything	**Despondency:** a sense that you cannot do it	
Daydreaming: staring into space, wishing to be elsewhere or that your goal is complete	**Temptation:** wanting to abandon your goal for something more interesting	
Habitual avoidance: switching focus elsewhere without consciously thinking about it	**Compulsive avoidance:** feeling unable to work on your goal, and yet also feeling bad, guilty, stressed or 'stuck'	

POINTS TO REMEMBER

Use the 'Working on your goal' exercise to guide you, and make notes using the BET record form if your motivation falters:

▶ Use a new BET record for each action block you attempt. This data will prove invaluable.

▶ Complete at least ten BET records before moving on to the next chapter.

▶ Ideally, complete the ten BET records across a number of sittings (your findings will be more representative).

You'll soon become familiar with the questionnaire part of the exercise.

Summary

Consider these points if you find yourself struggling:

1 If you forget about (or ignore) your goal, at least complete Part 1 of the questionnaire. This is just another demotivating challenge. Making notes about your experience will help you understand it.

2 Complete the questionnaire whenever you 'fail' miserably! You will learn important lessons and it will get easier.

3 If you feel overwhelmed by the questionnaire, put it into perspective: it often takes just seconds and you'll gain valuable insights.

4 If you *really* struggle, reread Chapters 2 and 3 and try again. Reconnect with your reasons for buying this book.

Making notes about the challenges you face may significantly boost your performance. You might even surprise yourself! Ultimately, you're just trying to do a bit of work and answer a few questions ... Do your best, and we can take it from there.

What I have learned

→ What are my thoughts, feelings and insights on what I have read so far?

_____

_____

_____

Use the space below to summarize any actions you identify as a result of reading this chapter.

_____

_____

_____

_____

Where to next?

 Identifying the demotivating challenges you face is the first step to overcoming them. Attempt some work on your goal and answer the questionnaire as directed. You might surprise yourself and work better than expected! If you struggle, do your best to record your experiences.

Complete the 'working on your goal' exercise ten times before moving on. In the next chapter we'll explore powerful new strategies for dealing with these challenges. For now, do your best and write up your findings.

8 Overcoming demotivating behaviour

In this chapter:

▶ you will identify different kinds of problematic demotivating behaviour

▶ you will learn why you should avoid such behaviour when working towards your goal

▶ you will discover two simple techniques designed to keep you on track.

In the previous chapter you were encouraged to work on your goal and to gather information by completing Exercise 15, 'Working on your goal'. Let's collate that information into something useful.

> **It's never too late to complete the exercises; you'll gain much more if you do.**

When working on your goal, did you manage to follow the four rules of valuing time?

1 Start when you're supposed to start.

2 Divide your time into 'action blocks' where necessary.

3 Work on your goal without distraction.

4 Take regular breaks promptly.

A high degree of motivation is unlikely at this stage, so we need to focus on the techniques that will help. We will begin by taking small, simple steps. Engage with the following exercises, and your motivation will improve.

→ Conflict and distraction

Did demotivated behaviour get the better of you? If so, what did you do instead? Let's identify the activities that threaten your motivation. For this next exercise, you will need your BET records from Chapter 7 to hand.

IDENTIFYING DEMOTIVATING CHALLENGES

This simple exercise takes one minute. The aim is to identify the activities that get in the way of your motivation.

 Read through the following checklist and tick any demotivated behaviour recorded on your BET records. There is space for your own suggestions if required.

Typical demotivating behaviours			
Enjoyable activities		**Social activities**	
Watching films, TV, DVDs	☐	Seeing friends or family	☐
Reading books, magazines, newspapers	☐	Making phone calls or sending texts	☐
Surfing the Internet	☐	Going out	☐
Browsing YouTube	☐	Spending time on social networking sites	☐
Listening to music	☐		
Playing computer games	☐		
Going shopping	☐		
Enjoying or reading about hobbies	☐		
Less important tasks		**Daydreaming and relaxing**	
Completing paperwork	☐	Thinking about the past or future	☐
Tidying the house	☐	Imagining a better life	☐
Checking emails	☐	Daydreaming about completing the task	☐
'Researching' related topics online	☐	Sitting or lying down, thinking	☐
Sorting through paperwork	☐	Coming up with plans and to-do lists	☐
'Organizing' things	☐	Going for a walk	☐
Exercising	☐		
Attending to personal grooming	☐		

Distractions		Your examples
Eating	☐	
Nail-biting	☐	
Worrying about problems	☐	
Smoking	☐	
Drinking	☐	
Taking drugs	☐	
Staring into space	☐	
Doing the opposite of my goal (e.g. eating instead of dieting)	☐	

Our aim isn't to stop you from enjoying yourself. These activities are often important to our wellbeing and stifling them would make little sense. However, allowing these activities to eat into your 'goal time' goes against your best interests. Success is a question of doing the right thing at the right time. Work on your goals first, and then enjoy these activities without guilt. Otherwise, you will come into repeated conflict.

→ Inconsistent behaviour

Making logical decisions is not always straightforward. For instance, experiments show that most people would choose five pounds now rather than (a guaranteed) ten pounds in two months' time. This makes little rational sense; effortlessly doubling your money is a great investment. The difficulty lies with our perception of *value*. Compared to the immediate moment, future rewards feel harder to grasp.

We are hard-wired to prefer the 'safer' option, which causes two problems. Your goals may seem *logically* rewarding, but their *emotional* value depends on your outlook. Feel certain you'll be genuinely rewarded and motivation increases. However, motivation weakens when the value of taking action is unclear. This is a problem when:

▶ we feel uncertain because we lack confidence

▶ rewards seem improbable because they're a long way off.

In either scenario, motivation falters because we cannot grasp the value of taking action.

There is a second difficulty. Prioritizing 'work' over enjoyment is difficult. Leaving your comfort zone requires effort and discipline. This grows even more frustrating when rewards are hard to value. Instead, we yearn for the easier option.

Motivation depends on *delaying gratification*. You will struggle to get anywhere without sacrificing lesser pleasures. Accept this truth and it sets you free. Here are some examples.

▶ You cannot watch reams of mindless TV and earn a good degree at the same time.

▶ You cannot eat bars of chocolate and enjoy feeling trim and healthy at the same time.

▶ You cannot spend your spare time in the pub and enjoy a good relationship with your family at the same time.

▶ You cannot shy away from conflict and build your confidence at the same time.

▶ You cannot leave mail unopened for days and be more organized at the same time.

These short-term activities hold much less value than the larger aim. We can rarely have both. Recognizing the value of taking action makes the sacrifices worthwhile. Life's pleasures become more enjoyable when savoured against a backdrop of success.

You previously identified your 'goal time'. The clue is in the name; there can be no room for conflict. Accept this truth and your motivation will double. This realism grants a single-minded focus. Internal conflicts then lessen.

> *'Nothing comes out of nothing.'*
>
> René Descartes

This next exercise creates a handy reference guide by highlighting the challenges you face. We'll add to it as we go along. If possible, keep it somewhere visible where you can easily refer to it.

Exercise 17

STARTING YOUR 'MOTIVATION FACT SHEET'

This exercise takes just a few minutes. It creates a document listing the demotivating challenges you face.

Begin by adding the title 'Motivation fact sheet' to a blank page in your notebook (alternatively, use a word processor).

Use your completed BET records to identify the following problems:

→ Did you sometimes start late? If so, write 'I did not start on time.'

→ Did you sometimes grow distracted? If so, write 'I became distracted.'

→ Did you take your breaks late? If so, write 'I did not take my breaks on time.'

→ Did you return late from your breaks? If so, write 'I did not return from breaks on time.'

Notice the use of the past tense. This helps people move beyond bad habits.

Next, write the subheading: 'Demotivating behaviours' and list the demotivating behaviours you ticked in Exercise 16.

1 _____

2 _____

3 _____

4 _____

Motivation fact sheet	
I sometimes struggle with motivation because:	Demotivating behaviours:
- I did not start on time	- Logging on to social networking sites
- I became distracted	- Checking my email
- I did not take my breaks on time	- Making snacks
- I did not return from breaks on time.	- Texting or calling friends.

We will add to this later. For now, refer to it often – ideally before you work on your goal. If necessary, type it up and email yourself a copy.

→ Demotivated behaviour: an addiction

When people become addicted to alcohol, their addiction eventually takes over. In response to certain cues, such as stress, boredom, certain times of the day or opportunity, their urge to drink is so overwhelming that free will gives way to blind compulsion. The same process applies to recovering smokers, drug addicts, workaholics, gambling addicts, Internet addicts, and similar.

Many researchers believe addiction is an emotionally charged habit. An alcoholic drinks because their *emotional mind* is attached to it and their *habitual mind* has automated it. When allied, these aspects of the mind are unstoppable.

As any recovering addict will affirm, there is no such thing as just once. Invariably, 'just once' leads to a resurgent addiction that quickly builds back to its uncontrollable worst. Cutting down rarely works. Only complete abstinence safeguards against relapse. This means accepting the addictive behaviour as impossible to control. The decision to avoid temptation is vitally important.

UNCONTROLLABLE DISTRACTION

Consider your own difficulties with motivation. Remember the wasted hours and the irrational decisions, the stress, excuses and missed opportunities. Ask yourself: can I control my demotivated behaviour – or does it control me?

Do you recognize the following?

▶ 'I'll just check my emails first.'

▶ 'I'll just quickly log on to Facebook.'

▶ 'I'll just have a quick read through the paper.'

▶ 'I'll just make a cup of tea.'

▶ 'I'll just have a snack first.'

▶ 'I'll just answer this text.'

▶ 'I just need to run to the shops first.'

Although seemingly innocuous, these decisions cause significant problems:

1 You sacrificed the important for the trivial. This is essentially an irrational decision.

2 These delays can spiral out of control: hour after hour stuck in the vortex of compulsive avoidance. Nothing is more miserable or frustrating.

3 Even minor delays add up; lost minutes eventually become lost hours.

The only way to be certain of preserving your motivation is to abstain from distraction. Contemplate this carefully if you frequently succumb to demotivated behaviour. It could change your life.

STEPS TO CONSIDER

To combat compulsive distraction, consider the following steps:

▶ Unplug the TV, the aerial, your games console and/or DVD player from the power socket.

▶ Switch off all electronic communications devices (even the vibrate function).

▶ Check emails and voicemails only at certain times. Log out of your email, Twitter, Facebook, Pinterest, etc.

▶ If certain websites are a problem, use a software-blocking tool like rescuetime.com to block them.

▶ Place your half-read novel in a cupboard somewhere.

You might think: 'Well, that's clearly unnecessary.' However, just as a recovering alcoholic must remove temptation because he knows 'just once' doesn't exist, one slip could completely ruin your day. Distraction *is* addictive.

In particular, be mindful when switching between different types of work. The change of pace destroys focus, and therefore motivation. Be extra vigilant during such moments.

Treat distraction as an addictive habit and you'll eradicate much heartache. Motivation then becomes much easier.

→ Strengthening motivation

Let's put these ideas into practice and work on your goal once more. This time, we're going to learn some simple skills through the following five exercises:

▶ Overriding demotivating challenges

▶ Tactical breathing

▶ Tuning into the challenge

▶ Taking action

▶ Quick review

These exercises will strengthen your motivation from the outset and help with demotivating challenges. In particular, watch out for the distracting behaviours identified earlier in this chapter.

Exercise 18

OVERRIDING DEMOTIVATING CHALLENGES

This exercise takes less than a minute. Use it in cases when you:

▶ are about to distract yourself

▶ are currently distracting yourself

▶ have just distracted yourself.

To begin, ask yourself: Am I avoiding taking action? This is a demotivating challenge. It's created by false messages sent by your brain. Unchecked, it will divert you from your best interests.

Breathe in deeply, exhale and *relax*... Accept the reality of your behaviour; identify what you'll lose as a result. For example:

➜ 'I was about to skip the gym rather than lose some weight.'

➜ 'I was messing around on the Internet rather than finishing my essay.'

➜ 'I just avoided calling the bank rather than sorting my overdraft.'

This type of statement dispels any illusions. To confirm any potential negative consequences, ask yourself:

➜ Will this avoidance make me happy now?

➜ Will it make me happy in the future?

➜ Is it worth sacrificing my goals for?

Rationally, the answer is always 'no'. Remember: demotivated behaviour is addictive. This moment is too important to leave to chance.

→ Imagine waking from a trance. If possible, stretch out your arms, take a deep breath, exhale and relax...

Use this simple exercise every time you need to ease past demotivating challenges. With practice, it will become an automatic response. You then become free to act in your best interests.

You do not have to give in to every demotivating challenge; you are much more than these signals. Let's put this new awareness to good use by focusing on what you can do.

All demotivated states depend on a fundamental lie: that your demotivated reality is your *only* reality. This is simply not true. At such times, try to switch your brain back on. The next exercise helps with that.

 # Exercise 19

TACTICAL BREATHING

This exercise takes 60 seconds or so. It relaxes your physiology, sheds stress and aids rational thought. Use this relaxation technique to combat the stress and frustration associated with taking action. Read through the steps first, to familiarize yourself with them.

Never use this exercise when your full concentration is required, e.g. when driving or operating machinery.

 Do you feel relaxed and ready for action? If not, we need to clear the decks. Look up slightly and close your eyes. Your eyelids might twitch, which is normal. (If you are in a public place and you cannot close your eyes, let them defocus instead.)

→ Next, slowly breathe in through your nose, mentally counting from one to five as you do so.

→ Then exhale through your mouth. Relax your shoulders, jaw, back, stomach, tongue and feet. Tell yourself: 'soften and relax'. Let go of all tension and resistance.

→ Complete ten breaths in total. Be patient, breathe slowly, and avoid 'going through the motions'.

→ If you still feel anxious or frustrated, complete ten more breaths (or more if necessary) until you feel relatively free of resistance.

This exercise just takes moments, so don't rush it – that's the very problem you're trying to overcome! Go slowly and complete all ten breaths each time. Your ability to relax *will* improve, as will your ability to think rationally.

A calm state is *the foundation* of solid motivation. Use this quick technique whenever starting work on your goal – it relaxes the body and focuses the mind. It takes just moments to complete, so avoid skipping past it or rushing through it.

TUNING INTO THE CHALLENGE

This exercise takes less than a minute. It connects you to time, consequence and purpose. Use it before working on your goal.

In Chapter 2 you completed Exercise 3, 'How much time do you really have?' Look at that diagram now. Accept your time as too precious to waste.

→ Confirm the time and date now. Remind yourself how much time you have left. Remember that you only get to spend this time once, and it will eventually run out. So choose wisely!

→ Where are you? What are you here to do? What is your 'motive'? Marry positive action to the present moment and you'll meet your needs in positive ways.

→ You will encounter demotivating challenges on the way. You may even be experiencing one now, but you do not have to give in to it.

→ How many demotivating challenges might you face today? Anticipate them, recognize them and ease through them. You'll get more things done *and* be happier in life.

Demotivating challenges are made strong only by *temptation*. Feel certain you'll override them and they weaken dramatically. We lose motivation when we feel 'in two minds' about something. Focus on using your time wisely *and* working towards your best interests. You will never get a second bite at today, so choose to make the most of it.

Exercise 21

TAKING ACTION

This simple exercise takes just seconds. It re-establishes conscious control. Use it whenever you need to take action.

Begin by asking yourself: 'How does it feel when I *know* I'm about to do something?'

→ Whatever your answer, look at your next task and think, 'That's right! I'm doing that now.' Feel relieved to act in your best interests. Action *is* success.

→ Without thinking or hesitating, nudge yourself forward and start on the task. Keep breathing deeply and stay calm.

→ You may get pulses of hesitation or reluctance. Breathe through them and don't stop. It *is* possible to take action *alongside* negative emotions. And once started, it's much easier to keep going.

→ Gradually put other things out of your mind and zoom in on the task. Stay relaxed and focused at the same time. Ease past frustration and lose yourself in the moment.

This simple exercise gets us moving. With practice, you will achieve this degree of control within seconds. Action *is* success.

We have all been dismissively told to 'Just do it!' but rarely are we shown how. Our ability to 'just do' anything depends entirely on our sense of control. These simple exercises will help. While this workbook focuses on building motivated feelings, positive action does not always depend on 'feeling' motivated. We can act *alongside* some negative emotion, and our capacity to do this will improve with practice.

Exercise 22

QUICK REVIEW

This exercise takes a couple of minutes. It reinforces motivation and establishes good habits. Use it whenever you have just finished working on your goal.

Begin by asking: 'What can I tidy up for the next minute?'

→ Spend a little time straightening up in whatever way possible. Keep it in perspective: it's just a single minute.

→ Now update your action plan if necessary. Feel satisfied as you cross items off your list.

→ Program your next goal times into your smartphone or online calendar. Set an audible alarm for each one. This is a great habit to get into.

→ Finally, acknowledge your efforts and the challenges you have overcome – no matter how imperfectly. Try to feel satisfaction; building motivation is not easy.

Focusing just on results causes problems, as does highlighting our imperfections. Instead, accept that self-motivation is challenging. Feel pleased with your efforts. The importance of this cannot be overstated.

Don't be hard on yourself if you become demotivated. These challenges reflect unconscious processes designed to override your control. It's akin to beating yourself up for blinking. Instead, resolve to learn new skills and enhance your approach.

That said, perhaps the most important point about demotivating challenges is that you do not have to give in to them. Resisting these challenges sometimes causes stress, but you can still take action – even while experiencing demotivated thoughts and feelings. Use tactical breathing (Exercise 19) to ease past such moments. They are just false signals created by your brain.

These exercises might seem a lot to introduce in one go, but they are really simple to carry out and you'll soon get the hang of them. Let's see how they fit together.

→ Working on your goal

As before, write down your ten next available 'goal times'. Leave the 'Number of blocks' field blank if not relevant.

Goal calendar (preview)			
1 Date & time		Number of blocks	
2 Date & time		Number of blocks	
3 Date & time		Number of blocks	
4 Date & time		Number of blocks	
5 Date & time		Number of blocks	
6 Date & time		Number of blocks	
7 Date & time		Number of blocks	
8 Date & time		Number of blocks	
9 Date & time		Number of blocks	
10 Date & time		Number of blocks	

Using your smartphone or online calendar, set an *audible* alarm for each of these times. (Please do not skip this step! This advice is repeated in every chapter.)

Other types of goal

As mentioned in Chapter 7, this workbook describes how to build sustained motivation. If your goal involves completing quick tasks or making motivated decisions, complete the exercises in this chapter by following the steps below.

You might find that the various exercises take longer than the task(s) you're trying to accomplish! However, use the techniques anyway and make notes on your experience. You will form powerful new habits that will transform your motivation in the long run.

HOW TO TAKE ACTION

Here's our new plan. As before, use the BET questionnaire to record your experience. This time, should your motivation weaken, practise the exercises as directed.

This process comes in three parts:

▶ Part 1 describes how to start working on your goal.

▶ Part 2 describes how to continue working on your goal.

▶ Part 3 describes how to take – and return from – your breaks.

Should things things go wrong at any stage, make notes about your experiences using the BET questionnaire below.

Our aim is to follow the four simple rules of valuing time:

1 Start when you're supposed to start.

2 Divide your time into 'action blocks' where necessary.

3 Work on your goal without distraction.

4 Take regular breaks promptly.

Rising to the challenge

If you struggle at any point, recognize this as a demotivating challenge. These exercises will help:

1 Start by overcoming demotivating challenges (Exercise 18).

2 Follow this with tactical breathing (Exercise 19).

3 Finally, take action (Exercise 21) to focus on your goal.

Then continue with the next step, according to the exercise below.

 Exercise 23

STAYING ON TRACK

This exercise takes 45–50 minutes (plus stoppages) each time. It encourages you to work on your goal and record any demotivated periods. Complete the exercise every time you attempt an 'action block'.

Part 1: starting on time

Try to start promptly; be where you need to be and have everything you need. Write the date and time, and the task you're working on next, on a new BET record (see below).

If you started late, consider the thoughts, feelings, habits and behaviour that stood in your way. Answer the questionnaire below, using Part 1 of your current BET record.

Now set a 45-minute timer and get off to a good start by completing the following steps. Take two minutes or so to do the following.

→ Read your compelling vision statement.

→ Read your goal statement.

→ Read your action plan: which task(s) should you work on next?

→ Do Exercise 19, Tactical breathing.

→ Do Exercise 20, Tuning into the challenge.

→ Do Exercise 21, Taking action.

Part 2: working on my goal

Start working on your goal – without distraction – for the remainder of your action block. If your resolve weakens, recognize this as a demotivating challenge. Use the exercises listed above to ease past it.

Each time you lose motivation for more than 60 seconds, use Part 2 of your current BET record to make notes, again using the questionnaire. Then refocus on your goal.

Part 3: taking prompt breaks

After 45 minutes, start a 15-minute timer and take your break immediately. Leave your work area and focus on something else for a spell. Let your mind cool down!

Return from your break after 15 minutes and be ready to start your next action block, if scheduled.

Again, recognize the temptation to skip breaks (or return from them late) as demotivating challenges; combat such moments using the exercises above. If you become demotivated around your breaks, complete Part 3 of your BET record using the questionnaire below.

→ If you intend to carry on working, start a new 45-minute timer and follow the steps above. Use a new BET record each time, and repeat the exercises as requested. Should you complete four continuous action blocks, take a longer 45-minute break.

→ When you have finished, complete the quick review (Exercise 22). It only takes a couple of minutes. Treat any reluctance as another demotivating challenge. Use your new techniques to ease past it.

Follow the steps carefully and it will all make sense. If you can start a 45-minute block now, then do so. Otherwise, come back to this page when your next goal time starts.

Here's the questionnaire to use if you grind to a halt.

BET questionnaire
1   What **behaviour** did you do instead of working on your goal?
2   What **emotions** did you feel about working on your goal?
3   What **thoughts** discouraged you? Did you excuse yourself from taking action? Did you think negatively about the task ahead?
4   Was any of this **habitual**? (Did you distract yourself without consciously deciding to do so?)

Answering these questions takes moments. Be brief, but try to record some detail.

What to do next

Take a moment to complete these exercises and refocus on your goal:

1 Start by overcoming demotivating challenges (Exercise 18).

2 Follow this with tactical breathing (Exercise 19).

3 Finally, take action (Exercise 21) to focus on your goal.

These techniques should get you moving again.

Use the following form to record your answers to the questions. As mentioned previously, you could photocopy it for multiple uses or copy it by hand into a page of your notebook.

```
╭┈┈┈┈┈┈┈┈┈┈┈┈┈┈┈┈┈┈┈┈┈┈┈┈┈┈┈┈┈┈┈┈┈┈┈┈┈┈┈┈┈┈┈┈╮
┊                    BET record                ┊
┊ Date:                                        ┊
┊ Task:                                        ┊
┊ Part 1: starting on time                     ┊
┊ Behaviour:                                   ┊
┊ Emotions:                                    ┊
┊ Thoughts:                                    ┊
┊ Habit (Y/N):                                 ┊
┊ Part 2: working on my goal                   ┊
┊ During:        1         2         3         ┊
┊ Behaviour:                                   ┊
┊ Emotions:                                    ┊
┊ Thoughts:                                    ┊
┊ Habit (Y/N):                                 ┊
┊ During:        1         2         3         ┊
┊ Behaviour:                                   ┊
┊ Emotions:                                    ┊
┊ Thoughts:                                    ┊
┊ Habit (Y/N):                                 ┊
┊ Part 3: taking prompt breaks                 ┊
┊ Start of break:         End of break:        ┊
┊ Behaviour:              Behaviour:           ┊
┊ Emotions:               Emotions:            ┊
┊ Thoughts:               Thoughts:            ┊
┊ Habit (Y/N):            Habit (Y/N):         ┊
╰┈┈┈┈┈┈┈┈┈┈┈┈┈┈┈┈┈┈┈┈┈┈┈┈┈┈┈┈┈┈┈┈┈┈┈┈┈┈┈┈┈┈┈┈╯
```

Keep your notes brief while identifying the thoughts, feelings, habits and behaviours behind any demotivated episodes. Tracking your distractions is really important; it builds awareness and often increases motivation.

POINTS TO REMEMBER

Attempt these new techniques as frequently as possible. Use Exercise 23, 'Staying on track', to guide you. Even if it feels a bit repetitive, try not to skip any of the steps. You are building powerful new habits.

Make notes, using the questionnaire, whenever your motivation falters.

- Use a new BET record for each action block you attempt. This data will prove invaluable.
- Complete at least ten BET records before moving on to the next chapter.
- Ideally, complete the ten BET records across a number of sittings (your findings will be more representative).

You'll soon become familiar with this process. It's very straightforward.

→ Demotivating challenges

Always be mindful of the demotivating behaviours identified earlier in this chapter. Have your motivation fact sheet to hand and, if you feel tempted by demotivating activities, remember that you do not have to give in to them. Use the exercises to intervene before switching away from your goal.

Here is a list of the various challenges you may face. Use this list when completing your BET records.

Potential challenges		
Demotivating behaviour	Demotivating emotions	Demotivating thoughts
Any activity other than working towards your goal	**Complacency:** *ignoring the importance of working towards your goal, e.g. 'I can't be bothered', or 'It's not important.'*	**Plausible excuses:** *thoughts that give you permission to focus elsewhere, despite not standing up to scrutiny, e.g. 'I don't have to do this yet', or 'I don't have everything I need.'*
Over-planning: *excessively planning action instead of taking action*	**Reluctance, tiredness, boredom, frustration, anxiety and feeling overwhelmed:** *abandoning your commitment to your goal*	**Value judgements:** *your appraisal of the tasks ahead, e.g. 'It's boring', or 'It's not going to be good enough.'*
General dithering: *present but not really doing anything*	**Despondency:** *a sense that you cannot do it*	
Daydreaming: *staring into space, wishing to be elsewhere or thinking that your goal is complete*	**Temptation:** *wanting to abandon your goal for something more interesting*	
Habitual avoidance: *switching focus elsewhere without consciously thinking about it*	**Compulsive avoidance:** *feeling unable to work on your goal, and yet also feeling bad, guilty, stressed or 'stuck'*	

Summary

Left unchecked, demotivating behaviour completely derails our efforts. You might believe that you can control it, but perhaps the evidence suggests otherwise. The best advice is to avoid it altogether. Your life will be easier *and* you will achieve much more. It helps to recognize the temptation to delay as especially destructive.

You're learning new skills; so don't expect perfection immediately. Relax, take your time, and practise the exercises as much as possible.

What I have learned

→ What are my thoughts, feelings and insights on what I have read so far?

_____

_____

_____

_____

_____

Use the space below to summarize any actions you identify as a result of reading this chapter.

_____

_____

_____

_____

_____

_____

Where to next?

 In the next chapter we will discuss stress, anxiety and frustration. These powerful emotions often cause low motivation. Before moving on, it is important to practise the exercises in this chapter until you can do them easily, and to complete at least ten BET records. In time, they will prove invaluable.

9 Overcoming stressful feelings

In this chapter:

▶ you will identify the negative emotions that weaken your motivation

▶ you will learn about stress, anxiety and frustration – and how they create inertia

▶ you will practise easing past demotivating challenges and maintaining greater motivation.

In the previous chapter, you identified problematic demotivating behaviour. If you intervene before such behaviour takes hold, you're more likely to sustain your motivation. With practice, you will find that this becomes quite straightforward.

In this chapter we'll focus on a powerful demotivating factor: stress. Although the pain of an unfulfilled life is real, it sometimes feels preferable to working on our goals. This is a simple illusion, however: stress can be overridden but future regret cannot.

Let's identify those emotions that weaken motivation. For the next exercise, you will need the BET records you completed previously.

> 'Today is the tomorrow you worried about yesterday.'
>
> Dale Carnegie

Exercise 24

IDENTIFYING NEGATIVE EMOTIONS

This exercise takes just a few minutes. It identifies emotion-based demotivating challenges.

Glance through the BET records from previous chapters. What negative emotions did you note? Collate every instance of negative emotion experienced, ordering them as follows.

→ Before starting my action time:

_____

→ While working on an action block:

_____

→ When returning from a break:

_____

Here is an example.

Before starting my action time	*Complacent, tired, despondent, despondent, despondent and complacent.*
While working on an action block	*Reluctant, fed up, frustrated, frustrated.*
When returning from a break	*Stuck, stuck, despondent, stuck*

List every instance – even when you are being repetitive, as in the above example.

 Has the same emotion cropped up three times or more for each stage? If so, tick the relevant box below.

Before working on my goal, I am sometimes demotivated due to:	
Complacency	☐
Temptation to do other things	☐
Tiredness, boredom or despondency	☐

Reluctance, frustration or anxiety	☐
Feeling stuck in a state of compulsive distraction	☐
While working on my goal, I am sometimes demotivated due to:	
Complacency	☐
Temptation to do other things	☐
Tiredness, boredom or despondency	☐
Reluctance, frustration or anxiety	☐
Feeling stuck in a state of compulsive distraction	☐
When restarting after a break, I am sometimes demotivated due to:	
Complacency	☐
Temptation to do other things	☐
Tiredness, boredom or despondency	☐
Reluctance, frustration or anxiety	☐
Feeling stuck in a state of compulsive distraction	☐

Nothing destroys motivation like the inability to ease past negative emotions. The first step is, as always, to build better awareness. With that in mind, let's update your motivation fact sheet.

Exercise 25

ADDING TO YOUR MOTIVATION FACT SHEET

This exercise takes just a few minutes. It updates the motivation fact sheet that you created in the previous chapter.

On your motivation fact-sheet document, where you listed demotivating behaviours, create three new headings:

→ When starting, I need to look out for these emotions

→ When working, I need to look out for these emotions

→ When restarting after a break, I should be wary of these emotions

Then list the demotivating emotions you identified in the checklist above. Here is an example expanded fact sheet.

Motivation fact sheet (example)	
I sometimes struggle with motivation because	*I do not start on time.* *I become distracted.* *I do not take my breaks on time* *I do not return from breaks on time.*
I need to avoid these behaviours	*Logging on to social networking sites* *Checking my email* *Making snacks* *Texting or calling friends*
When starting, I need to look out for these emotions	*Complacency*
When working, I need to look out for these emotions	*Reluctance, tiredness, boredom and despondency* *Frustration and anxiety*
When restarting after a break, I should be wary of these emotions	*Complacency* *The temptation to do other things*

Identifying demotivating challenges improves our ability to rise above them. However, this document only helps if you can see it! Refer to it often – ideally before working on your goal.

→ # Overcoming the stress of motivation

For many people, working on their goals goes something like this:

1 They try to do something productive...

2 Which then provokes anxiety or frustration...

3 They attempt to resist those negative feelings...

4 Which causes even more stress...

5 So their motivation starts to falter...

6 And eventually they give up.

Manage the stress of action effectively and your motivation will improve.

WHAT IS STRESS?

Situations *perceived* as threatening cause stress. Our heart rate increases, blood pressure rises, breathing quickens and certain hormones are released. This affects us physically, mentally and emotionally; thoughts become frantic and feelings overwhelm us. Unchecked, stress spirals quickly out of control.

Although helpful in dangerous situations, unwarranted stress holds us back. We cannot concentrate, our mood suffers, and motivation is lost. Chronic stress is debilitating.

When motivation is low, taking action seems especially stressful. We experience this as anxiety or frustration. Even when low motivation is caused by complacency, a person's relaxed demeanour soon evaporates when they are forced into taking action.

WHAT IS ANXIETY?

Anxiety is our response to an *imagined* threat. For instance, compare these scenarios:

▶ You're cornered by an angry-looking dog. You try to get away but it lopes after you, clearly intent on causing harm. Fear is a rational response, because the animal is a genuine threat.

▶ You pass somebody walking their dog. It approaches you, tail wagging, to find out who you are. Fear would be an irrational response, since you're clearly in no danger.

In the second example, the threat is imagined rather than real. However, because we experienced fear, we might then start avoiding dogs – and avoiding going out altogether. These are known as 'safety behaviours' and they focus on avoidance. Their relationship to demotivating challenges is clear.

In the same way, we often feel anxious before working on our goals. We worry about failure, imperfection or getting things wrong. Although often unwarranted, these fears destroy our motivation. This avoidance is the essence of anxiety.

FRUSTRATION AND MOTIVATION

Stress also leads to frustration, which is our response to perceived *restriction*.

▶ Frustration is being unable to do what you want.

▶ Frustration is finding things difficult, boring or pointless.

▶ Frustration is angry disappointment – because we lack control.

Frustration renders *everything* difficult. As our clarity weakens we grow increasingly short-tempered. Even basic tasks seem intolerable, and we might even give up entirely.

Of course, achieving goals in life is inherently frustrating. Trying to avoid that frustration only holds us back. And yet, sustained motivation depends on managing those frustrations while we work. Otherwise, we would eventually grind to a halt.

Frustration is subjective; we each have our preferences and tolerances. You might hate cleaning or washing up, but some people find it genuinely therapeutic. The frustration we feel depends on our view of a particular task: consider it arduous and it will be. Consider it enjoyable (or, at least, tolerable) and, again, it will be.

> **Achieving our goals is complicated enough without undue stress getting in the way. Learning to act *alongside* anxiety or frustration is vital. This means relaxing your state in the moment, and thinking clearly when making decisions.**

→ Relaxation is vital

It might seem paradoxical, but solid motivation depends on your ability to stay relaxed. You may think: 'But I haven't got time to relax!' However, try to avoid feeling fear or guilt. The following advice is important.

DEALING WITH DAY-TO-DAY STRESS

Life grows increasingly unsatisfactory when motivation is scarce. Stress levels increase and self-motivation becomes *even* more difficult. This vicious cycle ruins lives. To combat this, you must relax *regularly*. It may seem counterintuitive, but shedding stress actually improves your ability to work on your goals. Otherwise, frustration and anxiety will frequently derail you.

What do you do to unwind? Watching TV does not count: research suggests that staring at screens – TVs, smartphones, tablet devices and laptops – often makes people *more* stressed.

Here is a list of some relaxing activities:

- ☐ Learning to draw or paint
- ☐ Having a massage
- ☐ Yoga or t'ai chi
- ☐ Writing a letter to a friend (they'll be amazed, and you'll be pleased)
- ☐ Baking
- ☐ Listening to your favourite music
- ☐ Taking a long, warm shower
- ☐ Cleaning (amazingly, some people claim this to be 'therapeutic'!)
- ☐ Cycling
- ☐ Meditating
- ☐ Going on a slow walk
- ☐ Reading fiction
- ☐ Aromatherapy
- ☐ Listening to the radio
- ☐ Swimming
- ☐ Socializing with friends (for stress-relief purposes, this means no alcohol)
- ☐ Visiting a local park or feeding the ducks

What relaxing activities could you fit into your life? This list is far from exhaustive – research the alternatives if necessary. Remember: try to put irrational guilt to one side. Without regular relaxation, sustained motivation will prove more difficult than necessary.

Use the space below to note three relaxing activities you could do on a daily or weekly basis.

1 _____

2 _____

3 _____

Aim to relax thoroughly at least once a week. You might think: 'I don't have the time to relax! I can't afford it! I'd be wasting time!' Genuinely lacking the time to relax makes it twice as important to do so.

DEALING WITH SITUATIONAL STRESS

Sustaining our motivation means overriding demotivating challenges, which depends on gliding past anxiety or frustration. Again, relaxation is key. Reducing background stress helps tremendously, but you also need a tool to use *in the moment*.

In Chapter 8 you learned the tactical breathing exercise. This overrides stressful emotions and weakens the challenges we face. Master this skill and your motivation will increase.

A key point about relaxation is that you cannot *force* yourself to relax. You're not trying to float on clouds everywhere you go – although that does sound quite nice – but you can try to feel less bothered by everyday frustrations and anxieties. The more you relax, the easier action becomes.

→ Ideas into practice

You can now put these ideas into practice when you return to work on your goal once more. To build your new skills, keep practising the exercises introduced in the previous chapter:

▶ overriding demotivating challenges (Exercise 18).

▶ tactical breathing (Exercise 19)

▶ tuning into the challenge (Exercise 20)

▶ taking action (Exercise 21)

▶ quick review (Exercise 22).

In particular, use the tactical breathing exercise to ease past stress, frustration and anxiety. When your motivation weakens, intervene as directed and put yourself back on track. You do not need to give in to every challenge.

RETURNING TO YOUR GOAL

As before, write down your ten next available goal times.

Goal calendar (preview)			
1 Date & time		Number of blocks	
2 Date & time		Number of blocks	
3 Date & time		Number of blocks	
4 Date & time		Number of blocks	
5 Date & time		Number of blocks	
6 Date & time		Number of blocks	
7 Date & time		Number of blocks	
8 Date & time		Number of blocks	
9 Date & time		Number of blocks	
10 Date & time		Number of blocks	

Leave the 'Number of blocks' field blank if not relevant.

Using your smartphone or online calendar, set an audible alarm for each of these times. (Please do not skip this step! This advice is repeated in every chapter.)

Other types of goal

As mentioned in Chapter 7, this workbook describes how to build sustained motivation. If your goal involves completing quick tasks or making motivated decisions, complete the exercises in this chapter by following the steps below.

You might find the various exercises take longer than the task(s) you're trying to accomplish! However, use the techniques anyway and make notes on your experience. You will form powerful new habits that will transform your motivation in the long run.

HOW TO TAKE ACTION

Here's our new plan. As before, use the BET questionnaire to record your experience. This time, should your motivation weaken, practise the exercises as directed.

This process comes in three parts:

▶ **Part 1** describes how to start working on your goal.

▶ **Part 2** describes how to continue working on your goal.

▶ **Part 3** describes how to take – and return from – your breaks.

Should things things go wrong at any stage, make notes about your experiences using the BET questionnaire below.

Our aim is to follow the four simple rules of valuing time:

1 Start when you're supposed to start.

2 Divide your time into 'action blocks' where necessary.

3 Work on your goal without distraction.

4 Take regular breaks promptly.

Rising to the challenge

If you struggle at any point, recognize this as a demotivating challenge. These exercises will help:

▶ Start by overriding demotivating challenges (Exercise 18).

▶ Follow this with tactical breathing (Exercise 19).

▶ Finally, take action (Exercise 21) to focus on your goal.

Then continue with the next step, according to the exercise below.

GETTING BACK ON TRACK

This exercise takes 45–50 minutes (plus stoppages) each time. It encourages you to work on your goal and record any demotivated periods. Complete the exercise every time you attempt an 'action block'.

Part 1: starting on time

Try to start promptly; be where you need to be and have everything you need. Write the date and time, and the task you're working on next, on a new BET record (see below).

If you started late, consider the thoughts, feelings, habits and behaviour that stood in your way. Answer the questionnaire below, using Part 1 of your current BET record.

Now set a 45-minute timer and get off to a good start by completing the following steps. Take two minutes or so to do the following.

→ Read your compelling vision statement.

→ Read your goal statement.

→ Read your action plan: which task(s) should you work on next?

→ Do Exercise 19, Tactical breathing.

→ Do Exercise 20, Tuning into the challenge.

→ Do Exercise 21, Taking action.

Part 2: working on my goal

Start working on your goal – without distraction – for the remainder of your action block. If your resolve weakens, recognize this as a demotivating challenge. Use the exercises practised so far to ease past it.

Should you lose motivation for more than 60 seconds, answer the questionnaire below – this time using Part 2 of your current BET record. This information will prove invaluable. Then refocus on your goal.

Part 3: taking prompt breaks

After 45 minutes, start a 15-minute timer and take your break immediately. Leave your work area and focus on something else for a spell. Let your mind cool down!

Return from your break after 15 minutes and be ready to start your next action block, if scheduled.

Again, recognize the temptation to skip breaks (or return from them late) as demotivating challenges; combat such moments using the exercises above. If you become demotivated around your breaks, complete Part 3 of your BET record using the questionnaire below.

→ If you intend to carry on working, start a new 45-minute timer and follow the steps above. Use a new BET record each time, and repeat the exercises as requested. Should you complete four continuous action blocks, take a longer 45-minute break.

→ When you have finished, complete the quick review (exercise 22). It only takes a couple of minutes. Treat any reluctance as another demotivating challenge. Use your new techniques to ease past it.

Follow the steps carefully and it will all make sense. If you can start a 45-minute block now, then do so. Otherwise, come back to this page when your next goal time starts.

Here's the questionnaire to use if you grind to a halt.

BET questionnaire
1 What **behaviour** did you do instead of working on your goal?
2 What **emotions** did you feel about working on your goal?
3 What **thoughts** discouraged you? Did you excuse yourself from taking action? Did you think negatively about the task ahead?
4 Was any of this **habitual**? (Did you distract yourself without consciously deciding to do so?)

Answering these questions takes moments. Be brief, but try to record some detail.

What to do next

Take a moment to complete these exercises and refocus on your goal:

1 Start by overriding demotivating challenges (Exercise 18).

2 Follow this with tactical breathing (Exercise 19).

3 Finally, take action (Exercise 21) to focus on your goal.

These techniques should get you moving again.

Use the following BET form to record your answers to the questions. Here is a blank one to photocopy, or to copy by hand into a page of your notebook.

BET record

Date:

Task:

Part 1: starting on time

Behaviour:
Emotions:
Thoughts:
Habit (Y/N):

Part 2: working on my goal

During:	1	2	3
Behaviour:			
Emotions:			
Thoughts:			
Habit (Y/N):			

During:	4	5	6
Behaviour:			
Emotions:			
Thoughts:			
Habit (Y/N):			

Part 3: taking prompt breaks

Start of break:	**End of break:**
Behaviour:	Behaviour:
Emotions:	Emotions:
Thoughts:	Thoughts:
Habit (Y/N):	Habit (Y/N):

Continue to make brief notes on your experience. Pay attention to your thoughts, feelings, habits and behaviours whenever you feel demotivated.

POINTS TO REMEMBER

Attempt the exercises introduced in Chapter 8 as often as necessary. Use Exercise 26, Getting back on track, to guide you. Even if it feels a bit repetitive, try not to skip any of the steps. You are building powerful new habits.

Make notes, using the questionnaire, whenever your motivation falters.

▶ Use a new BET record for each action block you attempt. This data will prove invaluable.

- Complete at least ten BET records before moving on to the next chapter.
- Ideally, complete the ten BET records across a number of sittings (your findings will be more representative).

You'll soon become familiar with this process. It's very straightforward.

→ Demotivating challenges

Always be mindful of the demotivating behaviours identified earlier in this chapter. Have your motivation fact sheet to hand and, if you feel tempted by demotivating activities, remember that you do not have to give in to them. Use the exercises to intervene before switching away from your goal.

Here is the list of the various challenges you may face. Use it for reference when completing your BET records.

Challenges		
Demotivating behaviour	Demotivating emotions	Demotivating thoughts
Any activity other than working towards your goal	**Complacency:** ignoring the importance of working towards your goal, e.g. 'I can't be bothered', or 'It's not important.'	**Plausible excuses:** thoughts that give you permission to focus elsewhere, despite not standing up to scrutiny, e.g. 'I don't have to do this yet', or 'I don't have everything I need.'
Over-planning: excessively planning action instead of taking action	**Reluctance, tiredness, boredom, frustration, anxiety, and feeling overwhelmed:** abandoning your commitment to your goal	**Value judgements:** your appraisal of the tasks ahead, e.g. 'It's boring', or 'It's not going to be good enough.'
General dithering: present but not really doing anything	**Despondency:** a sense that you cannot do it	
Daydreaming: staring into space, wishing to be elsewhere or thinking that your goal is complete	**Temptation:** wanting to abandon your goal for something more interesting	
Habitual avoidance: switching focus elsewhere without consciously thinking about it	**Compulsive avoidance:** feeling unable to work on your goal, and yet also feeling bad, guilty, stressed or 'stuck'	

Summary

Easing past stress dramatically improves motivation. Use Exercise 19, Tactical breathing, to stay rational and in control. You're not trying to *eradicate* frustration or anxiety. Instead, try to feel undaunted by it. Achieving this aim opens a world of possibilities.

It's still early days, and there are challenges ahead. Relax, take your time, and keep practising the exercises.

What I have learned

→ What are my thoughts, feelings and insights on what I have read so far?

_____

_____

_____

Use the space below to summarize any actions you identify as a result of reading this chapter.

_____

_____

_____

_____

Where to next?

In the next chapter, we'll explore techniques to foster motivated thinking and planning. For now, practise the techniques introduced so far as much as possible. With repetition, they'll become second nature. Complete at least ten BET records before moving on to Chapter 10.

10 *Motivated thinking and planning*

In this chapter:

▶ you will learn how our moment-to-moment thinking affects our motivation

▶ you will discover powerful techniques designed to help you think positively about taking action

▶ you will learn how to draw up a 'next action' list – a document designed to foster clarity.

In the previous chapter you learned how to ease past stress. This key skill enables us to stay calm 'in the moment', rendering us less prone to distraction. Our motivation then improves because we make better decisions.

Next, let's explore how our thoughts about forthcoming tasks affect our motivation. For example, contrast this demotivated approach:

▶ Focus on the hassle of doing the washing up.

▶ Respond by feeling unenthusiastic and reluctant to do it.

▶ Avoid doing the washing up.

with a motivated approach:

▶ Imagine washing up quickly and easily.

▶ Respond by feeling willing to do it.

▶ Start doing the washing up.

This is a simple example, but the difference is clear. Your *focus* determines your willingness. Emphasize the negative and motivation weakens. Think in motivating terms and action becomes far easier.

→ Motivated thinking

To see motivated thinking in action, let's review another case study.

Janine's story

Janine had wanted to visit South America for as long as she could remember. She'd saved for many years and her plan was all in place. It was starting to feel real!

At the same time, Janine was also trying to learn Spanish. She set a SMART goal, created an action plan, and subscribed to an online course. Although the course came highly recommended, she ran into repeated difficulty.

This completely bewildered her. Janine felt so enthusiastic about her trip and knew speaking Spanish would help. And yet she found learning the language incredibly frustrating. Her motivation just repeatedly vanished.

Without realizing it, Janine's thoughts about the course were discouraging her. When sitting down to study, she would:

- imagine how long learning Spanish was going to take

- focus on the frustrations involved in the process

- forget about the rewards speaking Spanish would bring

- yearn to plan her trip instead – a far less stressful pastime.

Thoughts such as these could only destroy her motivation. She needed to see things differently. Here's how she did it:

- She concentrated on small chunks of work, which then felt less overwhelming.

- She resolved to engage with the process and focus on improving.

- She remembered the point of learning Spanish – to interact with the local people.

- Finally, she accepted the need to study rather than plan her trip for the thousandth time.

Janine soon got the hang of this and made excellent progress. Whenever her motivation wavered, she amended her thinking. Her enthusiasm would then return.

> *'All that we are is the result of what we have thought.'*
>
> Buddha

Janine's story shows how our thoughts determine the strength of our willingness. Imagining tasks to be long-winded, complex or pointless will only weaken our motivation. There is a better way; with practice, your thoughts can create focus and enthusiasm. It's a question of thinking *resourcefully*.

Some people say they enjoy going to the cinema but rarely seem to do so. They consider it a chore: arriving on time, queuing for a ticket, finding a seat, sharing space with others ... it all seems like too much bother. Others think differently: they focus on the enjoyable aspects of the experience and feel much more willing to go. The difference in motivation is clear. It depends on how you imagine the task or activity at hand.

Whether you think positively or negatively, your subsequent emotions will alter your motivation.

Exercise 27

MOTIVATED THINKING

This exercise takes around ten minutes. It will help you think more resourcefully about taking action. Use it whenever planning action.

The following techniques increase motivation by changing the way you consider upcoming action. Read through each one carefully.

Familiarize yourself with each technique. Then select a forthcoming task from your action plan and describe how each approach could apply. (Use the same task each time, or vary it – it is up to you.)

1 Put it into perspective

Do you habitually overestimate the effort an action will take? People often do. When feeling discouraged by something, ask yourself:

- ▶ How much time will this actually take?
- ▶ Is it really that difficult?
- ▶ Isn't there a point to this?

We often make snap judgements without realizing it. If we put things into perspective and consider the *actual* task at hand, we'll find that most things in life are not difficult – just unfamiliar. If you gain this perspective when 'weighing up' an action, your motivation will increase.

 Select a task from your action plan. Choose something you find daunting. How could you put it into perspective? Here's an example to start you off:

'When I struggle to feel motivated about washing up, I can remember that it only takes 20 minutes, and is a very easy job to do. It'll be over in no time!'

→ Write your example here:

_____

_____

Whenever you feel discouraged, check your assessment of the work ahead. The reality is often easier than we imagine, and putting things into perspective really helps.

2 Focus on small chunks

Organizing your time into action blocks helps, but you can break things down even further. You can do this using either *time* or *quantity*. Either way, focus on bite-sized chunks. Tell yourself:

- ▶ Let's just get the first 15 minutes out of the way.
- ▶ I'll just get this first bit done.
- ▶ I'll be fine when I'm up and running!

This approach reduces stress and fosters motivation because we feel less overwhelmed. Once up and running, you can then get into 'the zone'.

Again, select a task from your action plan. How could you break it into small chunks? What would you do first? Here's an example:

▶ 'When I don't know where to start on this essay, I can just focus on the first paragraph and get that right instead.'

→ Write your example here:

_____

_____

If you focus on small chunks rather than the unmanageable whole, you will feel more willing to take action.

3 Enhance your experience

It's easy to dwell on *the negatives*. However, it's easier to carry out a task when it's cast in a positive light. Get this right and you'll feel engaged by the moment. The hours will then fly by.

Of course, some tasks are impossible to love – ripping up carpets or filing a tax return, for example – but even here you can soften the blow. You could think: 'I'll listen to music while doing this', or 'I'll enjoy a cup of tea while I get on with it.' (However, avoid eating or drinking excessively while working; you'll only come to regret it!) Ask yourself:

▶ What could be enjoyable about this?

▶ Can I become more engaged with the task?

▶ Can I 'sweeten the pill'?

▶ Can I turn this into a game?

The following approaches can be very effective:

▶ **Focus on the enjoyable aspects.** Anyone can develop tunnel vision, so turn this to your advantage by focusing only on the more pleasurable aspects of a task. Action becomes easier because you enjoy it more. There are three stages to this:

1 *Anticipation*: look at the task ahead and 'pump yourself up'

2 *Action*: concentrate only on the enjoyable aspects of what you are doing or (at least) feel pleased for getting things done

3 *Reflection*: acknowledge your efforts and progress; this will make things easier in future.

- ▶ **Engage with the moment.** Relaxing and focusing are key. Try to put other thoughts to one side. Use the tactical breathing exercise if frustrations rise, and *do* rather than *think*. With practice, this approach is incredibly powerful. Engagement makes everything easier.
- ▶ **Sweeten the pill.** Make unpleasant jobs bearable by introducing pleasurable elements alongside them, e.g. studying to music, ironing in front of your favourite programme, catching up on emails in a coffee shop, exercising with friends, etc. Enhancing the experience makes taking action easier.
- ▶ **Make a game out of it.** As children, we routinely turn things into games. Tap into that ability and time will fly by – particularly with repetitive or boring tasks. Try cleaning against the clock or imagining that, if you complete your report by midday, that the gold medal will be yours...

Most tasks can be thought about in positive terms (admittedly not everything: tax returns will always be unpleasant!). Rather than feeling cynical or jaded, allow yourself to think positively. Your willingness will increase.

 Again, select a task from your action plan and apply one of the techniques above. Here's an example:

'When answering emails at home (which I hate), I'll imagine I'm actually having a conversation with people face to face (which I love!).'

→ Write your example here:

_____

_____

4 Create competition

Some people excel in competitions. It creates a benchmark to strive against, and winning always feels good. Creating competition could dramatically improve your motivation, so consider the following:

- ▶ Who am I competing against?
- ▶ I am going to do even better this time!
- ▶ I'll prove I can do this!

In the right circumstances, relaxed competition pushes us forward and we become less concerned with the effort things take. If you're naturally competitive anyway, this could give you an edge.

 Select a task from your action plan and consider how competition could help. Here's an example:

'Today in the gym I'm going to shave 20 seconds off my usual time.'

→ Write your example here:

_____

_____

5 Boost your energy

Feeling tired or hungover destroys motivation and often leads to uncontrollable distraction. If you frequently struggle to motivate yourself through tiredness or lethargy, try the following:

▶ **Drink two glasses of water quickly.**

▶ **Splash cold water on your face.**

▶ **Listen to loud music and dance around for five minutes.**

▶ **Eat a banana!**

▶ **Spend a bit of time decluttering something.**

Although it's not impossible, it is difficult to feel simultaneously tired and motivated. If low energy is a frequent problem for you, consider a health check-up, taking nutritional advice, and reviewing your sleeping patterns and your relationship with exercise.

In summary

Thinking positively about the tasks ahead will significantly improve your motivation. Reread the five ways to increase motivation listed above and familiarize yourself with each approach. Can you now think differently about your action plan? Keep an open mind and explore the possibilities. We will put these techniques into action shortly.

Most people are motivated in one area of their life. Most likely, this is because they enjoy it. If you can relate to this, figure out how it motivates you. Bring that style of thinking into play elsewhere.

→ 'Next action' planning

Another key method for boosting motivation is 'next action' planning.

Confusion creates demotivated behaviour; we grow fuzzy-minded and grind to a halt. People who plan their actions make better progress, because motivation depends on knowing what to do next.

The following exercise involves drawing up a list of your 'next actions' – the steps needed to complete a given task. Your next action list is a disposable document; you jot notes in your notebook and then get to work. It needn't be too involved.

However, try not to gloss over it. Next action planning breaks tasks into bite-sized chunks. It's another important addition to your motivation toolbox.

 *Exercise 28*

PLANNING YOUR NEXT ACTIONS

This exercise takes a minute or so. It helps you plan your 'next actions'. Use it before taking action.

 Note the time and date and read through your action plan. What do you need to do next?

→ Does a time-sensitive task need completing urgently?

→ Is there an order-sensitive task that needs completing next?

→ If not, either select the largest job or warm up first (by completing a few quick tasks).

Select a task and break it into bite-size chunks. Describe *what* you need to do – and *how*. Keep each step under 15 minutes, if possible. Plan for the next 45 minutes or so.

Then, organize these steps into the order you'll complete them by numbering each one (see the example below).

How can you think positively about the work ahead? Try to be specific.

→ Do I need to put it into perspective?

→ What could be enjoyable about this?

→ How can I become engaged with these tasks?

→ Can I 'sweeten the pill'?

→ Can I turn this into a game?

→ Can I create competition?

→ Do I need to boost my energy?

Keep it simple. Try just one or two techniques. Go with something appropriate for the task(s) you're working on. Only take a moment to sketch out this list, as in the following example.

Example 'next actions' list	
13 December Task: complete Chapter 2	Think positively by:
Revise the opening paragraph by trimming out repeated points. ① Copy referencing information from the previous notes. ③ Plan chapter framework by referring to Chapter 1. ②	Listening to music Feel engaged, as if I'm talking to friends about the subject

Notice how these actions cover the *what* and the *how*. Imagine describing the task to somebody else; break it into small chunks and state what needs doing.

As you progress through your list, tick off each action. It will feel satisfying!

→ # Ideas into practice

Let's put these new ideas to the test. You're again advised to work on your goal and practise planning your 'next actions' using the exercises in this chapter. Break upcoming tasks into smaller steps, and work out how you'll think positively about it.

To build your skills, keep practising the exercises introduced in Chapter 8:

- ▶ overriding demotivating challenges (Exercise 18).
- ▶ tactical breathing (Exercise 19)
- ▶ tuning into the challenge (Exercise 20)
- ▶ taking action (Exercise 21)
- ▶ quick review (Exercise 22).

When your motivation weakens, intervene as directed and put yourself back on track. You do not need to give in to every challenge.

RETURNING TO YOUR GOAL

As before, write down the next ten times you will work on your goal.

Goal calendar (preview)			
1 Date & time		Number of blocks	
2 Date & time		Number of blocks	
3 Date & time		Number of blocks	
4 Date & time		Number of blocks	
5 Date & time		Number of blocks	
6 Date & time		Number of blocks	
7 Date & time		Number of blocks	
8 Date & time		Number of blocks	
9 Date & time		Number of blocks	
10 Date & time		Number of blocks	

Leave the 'Number of blocks' field blank if not applicable.

Using your smartphone or online calendar, set an audible alarm for each of these times. (Please do not skip this step! This advice is repeated in every chapter.)

Other types of goal

As mentioned in Chapter 7, this workbook describes how to sustain motivation because people find that the most challenging. If your goal involves completing quick tasks or making motivated decisions, follow the steps below.

HOW TO TAKE ACTION

As before, use the BET questionnaire to record your experience. This time, should your motivation weaken, practise the exercises as directed.

This process comes in three parts:

▶ **Part 1** describes how to start working on your goal.

▶ **Part 2** describes how to continue working on your goal.

▶ **Part 3** describes how to take – and return from – your breaks.

Should things things go wrong at any stage, make notes about your experiences using the BET questionnaire below.

Our aim is to follow the four simple rules of valuing time:

1 Start when you're supposed to start.

2 Divide your time into 'action blocks' where necessary.

3 Work on your goal without distraction.

4 Take regular breaks promptly.

> If you struggle for motivation at any point, recognize this moment as a demotivating challenge. These exercises will help:
>
> 1 Start by overriding demotivating challenges (Exercise 18).
>
> 2 Follow this with tactical breathing (Exercise 19).
>
> 3 If confused, check your 'next action' list. Is the next step clear?
>
> 4 Finally, take action (Exercise 21) to focus on your goal.
>
> Then continue with the next step, according to the exercise below.

WORKING ON YOUR GOAL

This exercise takes 45–50 minutes (plus stoppages) each time. It encourages you to work on your goal and record any demotivated periods. Complete the exercise every time you attempt an 'action block'.

Part 1: starting on time

Try to start promptly; be where you need to be and have everything you need. Write the date and time, and the task you're working on next, on a new BET record (see below).

If you started late, consider the thoughts, feelings, habits and behaviour that stood in your way. Answer the questionnaire below, using Part 1 of your current BET record.

Now set a 45-minute timer and get off to a good start by completing the following steps. Take two minutes or so to do the following.

→ Read your compelling vision statement.

→ Read your goal statement.

→ Read your action plan: which task(s) should you work on next?

→ Do Exercise 19, Tactical breathing.

→ Do Exercise 20, Tuning into the challenge.

→ Do Exercise 28, Planning your next actions.

→ Do Exercise 21, Taking action.

Part 2: working on my goal

Start working on your goal – without distraction – for the remainder of your action block. If your resolve weakens, recognize this moment as a demotivating challenge. Use the exercises listed above to ease past it.

Should you lose motivation for more than 60 seconds, answer the questionnaire below – this time using Part 2 of your current BET record. This information will prove invaluable. Then refocus on your goal.

Part 3: taking prompt breaks

After 45 minutes, start a 15-minute timer and take your break immediately. Leave your work area and focus on something else for a spell. Let your mind cool down!

Return from your break after 15 minutes and be ready to start your next action block, if scheduled.

Again, recognize the temptation to skip breaks (or return from them late) as demotivating challenges; combat such moments with the exercises above. If you become demotivated around your breaks, complete Part 3 of your BET record using the questionnaire below.

→ If you intend to carry on working, start a new 45-minute timer and follow the steps above. Use a new BET record each time, and repeat the exercises as requested. Should you complete four continuous action blocks, take a longer 45-minute break.

→ When you have finished, complete the quick review (Exercise 22). It only takes a couple of minutes. Treat any reluctance as another demotivating challenge. Use your new techniques to ease past it.

Follow the steps carefully and it will all make sense. If you can start a 45-minute block now, then do so. Otherwise, come back to this page when your next goal time starts.

Here's the questionnaire to use if you grind to a halt.

BET questionnaire	
1	What **behaviour** did you do instead of working on your goal?
2	What **emotions** did you feel about working on your goal?
3	What **thoughts** discouraged you? Did you excuse yourself from taking action? Did you think negatively about the task ahead?
4	Was any of this **habitual**? (Did you distract yourself without consciously deciding to do so?)

Answering these questions takes moments. Be brief, but try to record some detail.

What to do next

Take a moment to complete these exercises and refocus on your goal:

1 Start by overriding demotivating challenges (Exercise 18).

2 Follow this with tactical breathing (Exercise 19).

3 Finally, take action (Exercise 21) to focus on your goal.

These techniques should get you moving again.

As before, use the following form to record your answers to the questions.

BET record

Date:

Task:

Part 1: starting on time

Behaviour:
Emotions:
Thoughts:
Habit (Y/N):

Part 2: working on my goal

During:	1	2	3
Behaviour:			
Emotions:			
Thoughts:			
Habit (Y/N): 123			

During:	4	5	6
Behaviour:			
Emotions:			
Thoughts:			
Habit (Y/N):			

Part 3: taking prompt breaks

Start of break:	**End of break:**
Behaviour:	Behaviour:
Emotions:	Emotions:
Thoughts:	Thoughts:
Habit (Y/N):	Habit (Y/N):

Keep your notes brief while identifying the thoughts, feelings, habits and behaviours behind any demotivating challenges. Tracking these distractions continues to build motivation.

POINTS TO REMEMBER

Use the 'Planning your next actions' exercise each time you work on your goal. Also, continue to practise the exercises introduced in Chapter 8. Use Exercise 29, 'Working on your goal', to guide you. Keep building your powerful new habits!

Use the questionnaire to make notes whenever your motivation falters.

▶ Use a new BET record for each action block you attempt. This data will prove invaluable.

▶ Complete at least ten BET records before moving on to the next chapter.

▶ Ideally, complete the ten BET records across a number of sittings (your findings will be more representative).

You'll soon become familiar with this process. It's very straightforward.

→ Demotivating challenges

Look out for discouraging thoughts ahead of taking action. Engage in motivated thinking, and break everything down into small chunks. This way, you should avoid feeling overwhelmed.

Keep up the habit of gently guiding yourself towards your best interests. Pay extra attention when you feel stressed, frustrated or anxious, or when you are tempted by the demotivating behaviours identified in Chapter 8. Have your motivation fact sheet to hand, and use the various exercises to stay on track as best you can.

Here is a list of the various challenges you may face. Use this list when completing your BET records.

Challenges		
Demotivating behaviour	Demotivating emotions	Demotivating thoughts
Any activity other than working towards your goal	**Complacency:** ignoring the importance of working towards your goal, e.g. 'I can't be bothered', or 'It's not important.'	**Plausible excuses:** thoughts that give you permission to focus elsewhere, despite not standing up to scrutiny, e.g. 'I don't have to do this yet', or 'I don't have everything I need.'
Over-planning: excessively planning action instead of taking action	**Reluctance, tiredness, boredom, frustration, anxiety, and feeling overwhelmed:** abandoning your commitment to your goal	**Value judgements:** your appraisal of the tasks ahead, e.g. 'It's boring', or 'It's not going to be good enough'.
General dithering: present but not really doing anything	**Despondency:** a sense that you cannot do it	
Daydreaming: staring into space, wishing to be elsewhere or thinking that your goal is complete	**Temptation:** wanting to abandon your goal for something more interesting	
Habitual avoidance: switching focus elsewhere without consciously thinking about it	**Compulsive avoidance:** feeling unable to work on your goal, and yet also feeling bad, guilty, stressed or 'stuck'	

Summary

Relax, take your time, and think positively about the tasks ahead. By planning your next actions, you're fostering greater purpose. Smaller chunks are easier to manage. When combined with motivated thinking, your clarity and enthusiasm should improve. Spend only a minute or two on the planning process: keep it rough and ready.

What I have learned

→ What are my thoughts, feelings and insights on what I have read so far?

_____

_____

_____

Use the space below to summarize any actions you identify as a result of reading this chapter.

_____

_____

_____

_____

Where to next?

In the next chapter we will explore the broader negative mindsets behind low motivation. In the meantime, keep practising, and complete ten BET records before moving on to the next chapter.

11 Overcoming a negative mindset

In this chapter:

▶ you will learn about negative mindsets and how they hold us back
▶ you will explore the limiting rules, beliefs and assumptions that destroy motivation
▶ you will practise a technique designed to reverse a negative mindset and shed your emotional 'baggage'.

Our mindset is governed by certain beliefs. These beliefs affect how we view the world around us. When an irrational mindset holds sway, our whole experience changes. We grow anxious, despondent, and even helpless. Motivation gives way to fear and inertia.

Although irrational, our mindset creates our reality. In this chapter, we will explore techniques to restore your freedom. If you can clear your mind, your ability to take action will increase and you will regain your sense of control.

Overcoming a negative mindset depends on seeing past irrational thinking. Fear, frustration, complacency and despondency will then tend to abate. The key is learning to recognize negativity before it takes hold. The next exercise will help.

If you identify with any of these negative thoughts or feelings, the techniques in this chapter will help you overcome them.

'*What would life be if we had no courage to attempt anything?*'

Vincent van Gogh

Exercise 30

IDENTIFYING A LIMITING MINDSET

This exercise takes five to ten minutes. It will give you greater insight into your limiting mindsets. You will need your BET records from the previous chapters.

With your BET records to hand, read through the following list of typical demotivating assumptions. For each entry, ask yourself: 'Do I sometimes believe this when I'm feeling demotivated?' Tick any that you truly identify with.

Then give examples of any thoughts, feelings or situations that you have experienced recently.

'I must not fail.'

Many people fear the *idea* of failure, but some will do anything to avoid it. They predict catastrophic outcomes and profound disapproval, and worry incessantly about how they will cope.

This fear completely distorts perception. It compels us to avoid:

▶ **anything taking us out of our 'comfort zone'**
▶ **anything involving examination, judgement or scrutiny of us.**

A fear of failure often creates self-sabotaging behaviour. Holding ourselves back means that we can tell ourselves: 'It's okay because I didn't really try.' This only ever leads to disappointment.

Typical thoughts when fearing failure

It won't be good enough!	☐
I must get this right.	☐
It's not good enough – it's ruined.	☐
Oh dear, they'll think I'm stupid.	☐
I'm going to mess this up.	☐
Nobody else can ever see this.	☐
I could have done it, but I didn't try.	☐
I know I'm going to fail.	☐

Typical feelings when fearing failure

Fear and anxiety ☐

Strongly resisting trying action ☐

Feeling strongly pessimistic ☐

→ Write your own examples here:

1 _____

2 _____

3 _____

4 _____

5 _____

This fear is the most common cause of demotivated behaviour. However, the 'failure' we fear is rarely as bad as we imagine. Reversing this limiting mindset is essential for a happier life, because our avoidance of failure makes failure more likely.

'It has to be perfect.'

Our fears sometimes create an irrational desire for perfection. We imagine it will shield us against failure and rejection. Unfortunately, we then wilt under the pressure it causes. We know perfection is impossible, and we feel discouraged even before starting.

Perfectionism can be subtle. For instance, we might delay eating healthily due to a planned indulgent meal next week, despite the benefits we'd experience in the interim. Perfectionism also sometimes causes over-preparation. Although taking care is important, agonizing over every detail just wastes time. This lack of conviction really holds us back.

Typical thoughts when fearing imperfection

It has to be perfect. ☐

I need to get this right. ☐

This is terrible; I need to start from scratch. ☐

Why is it not good enough? ☐

I don't want to do it. ☐

I might as well just give up. ☐

Typical feelings when fearing imperfection

A strong sense of anxiety ☐

A strong feeling of resistance when trying to take action ☐

A yearning to do something less stressful ☐

A strong feeling of disappointment ☐

A desire to start again from scratch ☐

➡ Write your own examples here:

1 _____

2 _____

3 _____

4 _____

5 _____

Perfectionism causes needless anxiety and wastes time. Our work can never be perfect, but it can be good enough.

'Things must not change.'

Without realizing it, we assume that change will only bring difficulty. Inaction then becomes our refuge. We might not understand this consciously, but it is noticeable when even the smallest actions are rejected.

Typical thoughts when fearing change

Let's just do that later. ☐

I need to prepare properly – what if it all goes wrong? ☐

Something bad is going to happen; I can feel it. ☐

If I solve this problem, something bad is bound to happen. ☐

It's not worth the risk. ☐

This could turn out really badly. ☐

Let's just leave it for now. ☐

Typical feelings when fearing change

Fear and anxiety ☐

A strong feeling of resistance when trying to take action ☐

A yearning for things to stay the same ☐

A sense of pessimism, as if something bad is going to happen ☐

→ Write your own examples here:

1 _____

2 _____

3 _____

4 _____

5 _____

The problem here is simple. Inertia wastes time – your most precious resource.

'I must not succeed.'

It seems strange to think that people fear success, but this anxiety is very real. People worry about jealousy or unwanted attention – or that loved ones will be left behind. Additionally, success could then lead to more responsibility. This is the 'fear of failure' once more, and the same principles apply.

Typical thoughts when fearing success

I don't want to do this.   ☐

I'm worried about what people will think.   ☐

Doing this will just make everything worse.   ☐

Typical feelings when fearing success

Fear and anxiety   ☐

A strong feeling of resistance when trying to take action   ☐

A sense of pessimism, as if something bad is going to happen   ☐

→ Write your own examples here:

1 _____

2 _____

3 _____

4 _____

5 _____

This limiting mindset reflects a lack of confidence. In reality, we are more capable than we imagine. Achieving goals boosts our ability to deal with life. This includes managing our successes.

'Pleasure must come first.'

Imagine returning home from a busy day at work. You recently enrolled on a home study course and have lots of reading to do. Would you like to:

▶ study?

▶ do *anything* other than study?

Over-prioritizing pleasure leaves us vulnerable to distraction. We resort to bargaining and excuses, e.g. 'I'll start as soon as I've finished watching this...' Unfortunately, delay only ever creates more delay. Sometimes over-prioritizing pleasure is an *avoidance* tactic, masking a fear of failure or change. Either way, reversing this mindset is vital; otherwise, life becomes quite shallow.

Typical thoughts when pleasure comes first

I'll just enjoy this *other activity* first, and then I'll make a start. ☐

Life is too short to be doing this. ☐

I don't want to miss out! ☐

Life is for living – it should be fun! ☐

This is so boring. Let's do something else. ☐

Typical feelings when pleasure comes first

A *yearning* to do something more interesting at that moment ☐

Frustration at having to do something dull or routine ☐

A sense of missing out ☐

Curiosity about another experience that leads away from a pressing task ☐

→ Write your own examples here:

1 _____

2 _____

3 _____

4 _____

5 _____

Achieving your goals requires sacrifice. This does not mean becoming a fun-free drone, but attending to your responsibilities first *will* improve your experiences in life.

'I can't do it' or 'I don't know where to start!'

Low confidence distorts our thinking. We overestimate challenges and give up all too easily. We lose the chance to learn and continue to hold ourselves back.

These problems are compounded by an unforgiving personal attitude. We judge ourselves in the harshest possible terms – growing angry, pessimistic and despairing. Being patient with yourself is important, especially when you are learning new things.

Typical thoughts when a person believes it's too difficult

I can't do it. ☐

It's too hard. ☐

I'm no good at this. ☐

I don't have enough willpower. ☐

Why bother starting? ☐

Everyone will know I'm useless. ☐

Typical feelings when a person believes it's too difficult

A strong sense of anxiety and frustration ☐

A strong feeling of resistance when trying to take action ☐

A feeling that we're about to make a fool of ourselves ☐

A yearning to avoid the task ☐

➜ Write your own examples here:

1 _____

2 _____

3 _____

4 _____

5 _____

Everyone has to start somewhere. You'll only improve by giving things a go. Most tasks in life are not that difficult (just unfamiliar). Remembering this helps.

'I'm too tired' or 'I'm too stressed.'

It's hard to concentrate when we're not in the mood. Taking action *can* be frustrating, and tiredness and stress do not help. Motivation depends on our state of mind. However, it is still possible to work on your goal. Either stoke up your desire or, if necessary, act *alongside* negative feelings. With just a little practice, either approach is effective.

Typical thoughts when not in the mood to act

I'm too tired. ☐

I'm too stressed. ☐

I'm too anxious. ☐

I work better when I'm fresh. ☐

Typical feelings when not in the mood to act

A strong sense of frustration ☐

A strong feeling that there is no point in starting yet ☐

A desire to delay or abandon the task ☐

➜ Write your own examples here:

1 _____

2 _____

3 _____

4 _____

5 _____

Although stress and tiredness seem to get in the way, we could take action if we wish. Don't let these factors become excuses. The techniques in this chapter will help.

'I can't work like this.'

External factors can weaken our motivation. It could be too noisy or cold; you might not have enough time; you might not have everything you need; or your workspace could be quite messy. And yet you could still make a start if you tried. The problem with this thinking is that conditions may never be 'just right'.

Typical thoughts when conditions are 'unsuitable'

I've not got enough time to start now. ☐

I've not got everything I need. ☐

I need to take care of this before I start. ☐

There is no point starting this now. ☐

It's too noisy/quiet/cold/warm, etc. ☐

I need to wait until things are right. ☐

I can't work like this. ☐

I'll start tomorrow/after the weekend/after my birthday, etc. ☐

Let's just wait until conditions are more suitable. ☐

Typical feelings when conditions are 'unsuitable'

A strong sense of lethargy ☐

A strong feeling of resistance when trying to take action ☐

A desire to sort out a pressing problem other than the task you're procrastinating over ☐

A yearning to wait until circumstances are more conducive ☐

➜ Write your own examples here:

1 _____

2 _____

3 _____

4 _____

5 _____

As with tiredness or stress, we sometimes use unfavourable conditions as an excuse. Improving your motivation means changing this. Ultimately, you are only fooling yourself.

'I have plenty of time' and 'I work best under pressure.'

People often claim to work best under pressure and there is usually some truth in this. We work effectively when deadlines loom because the consequences of inaction are clear. The pressure gets us moving. However, this strategy is flawed: leaving everything to the last minute increases stress and leaves little room for error. The quality of our work often suffers, which we come to regret later on.

This sometimes suits our needs because we have a get-out clause: 'I could have achieved more if I'd spent more time on it.' We feel this protects us from failure, but it's a bitter comfort.

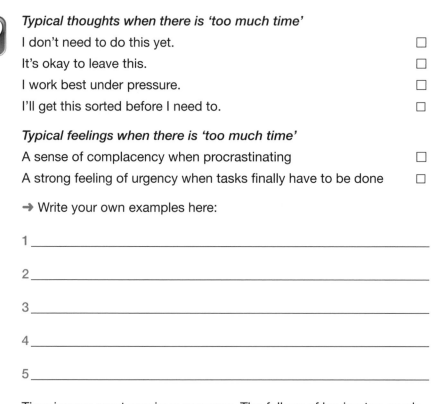

Typical thoughts when there is 'too much time'

I don't need to do this yet. ☐

It's okay to leave this. ☐

I work best under pressure. ☐

I'll get this sorted before I need to. ☐

Typical feelings when there is 'too much time'

A sense of complacency when procrastinating ☐

A strong feeling of urgency when tasks finally have to be done ☐

➜ Write your own examples here:

1 _____

2 _____

3 _____

4 _____

5 _____

Time is your most precious resource. The fallacy of having too much time is the most irrational assumption on this list.

'I hate being told what to do.'

Some people resent receiving instructions from others. Wilfulness takes over and we sabotage our efforts, even when it's irrational to do so. Motivation gives way to sulky resistance, which gets us nowhere.

Typical thoughts when we hate being told what to do

Why do I have to do this? ☐

This is pointless. ☐

I shouldn't have to do this just because I've been told to. ☐

I shouldn't have to do things I don't want to do. ☐

I'll show them; I'm just not doing it. ☐

I *hate* being told what to do! ☐

Typical feelings when we hate being told what to do

A strong sense of resentment ☐

A strong feeling of resistance when trying to take action ☐

A yearning to abandon the task, to send a message ☐

→ Write your own examples here:

1 _____

2 _____

3 _____

4 _____

5 _____

You might hate being told what to do, but our goals often depend on co-operation. Overcoming this resentment is important, and your life will be happier if you manage it.

In summary

Do any of these mindsets seem familiar? If so, overcoming them will improve your motivation. It's all a question of perception. Although they feel real in the moment, these mindsets are subjective, irrational and destructive.

→ # Ideas into practice

Let's put these new ideas to the test. You're again advised to work on your goal. We'll introduce a new technique: 'reversing a negative mindset'. Use it whenever you recognize the thoughts and feelings from this chapter. It is particularly effective when used before taking action.

To build your skills, keep practising the exercises introduced in previous chapters:

▶ overriding demotivating challenges (Exercise 18).

▶ tactical breathing (Exercise 19)

▶ tuning into the challenge (Exercise 20)

▶ planning your next actions (Exercise 28)

▶ taking action (Exercise 21)

▶ quick review (Exercise 22).

When your motivation weakens, intervene as directed and put yourself back on track. You do not need to give in to every demotivating challenge. Persevere with the exercises, and you'll retrain your approach to your life.

REVERSING A NEGATIVE MINDSET

This exercise takes a couple of minutes. It will reverse a negative mindset and create freedom. Use it whenever you are strongly resistant towards taking action.

For maximum impact, use tactical breathing (Exercise 19) first.

1 Identify your current negative mindset from the list below. If you recognize two or three, choose the one that stands out.

☐ I must not fail.

☐ It has to be perfect.

☐ Things must not change.

☐ I must not succeed.

☐ Pleasure must come first.

☐ I cannot do it.

☐ I am too tired/stressed.

☐ I cannot work like this.

☐ I have plenty of time/I work best under pressure.

☐ I hate being told what to do.

If uncertain, go with 'I must not fail.'

2 How would things change if you adopted the *opposite* mindset?

☐ I'd prefer not to fail, which means staying relaxed and motivated.

☐ Being 'good enough' is okay.

☐ Change is safe.

☐ Success is safe.

☐ Pleasure will come later.

☐ I can get better at this.

☐ I can do this even when tired or stressed.

☐ I'd prefer not to work like this, but I can choose to do it.

☐ My time is valuable/I don't need pressure to perform.

☐ I accept the need to co-operate when it's in my best interests.

3 Describe this new mindset below (or in your notebook). Imagine the thoughts and feelings you'd experience and the actions you'd undertake. Here are some clues:

▶ Feeling calm, happy, relaxed, and focused on your best interests

▶ Free from resistance or temptation

▶ Aware that there is nothing stopping you from acting now

▶ Engaged behaviour in the moment

→ Thoughts: _____

_____

→ Feelings: _____

_____

→ Actions: _____

_____

4 Next, we're going to 'pretend' you possess this resourceful mindset. Give yourself permission to do this (sometimes we believe pretending is pointless or forbidden).

→ Allow yourself to use your imagination – it is an incredibly powerful tool.

→ Put yourself into this resourceful state of mind.

→ Anticipate feeling different, weird, or 'out of your comfort zone'. This means that the exercise is working.

5 For the next 60 seconds, close your eyes (if possible; otherwise defocus them) and imagine holding this positive mindset.

→ Stay relaxed and conjure up the thoughts and feelings you'd experience.

→ Imagine having the freedom to focus solely on your best interests. Let yourself really get into it.

6 Check to make sure:

→ Is this new mindset useful?   Yes/No

→ Will it combat distraction and inertia?   Yes/No

→ Does it open new possibilities?   Yes/No

→ Is it healthy and safe to think like this?   Yes/No

7 If the answer to these questions is yes, continue with this mindset as you work on your goal.

This new mindset should be happier, easier, and more productive than before. Staying positive, relaxed and *free* helps people think clearly and achieve their goals. You have nothing to lose.

Your limiting mindsets are emotional baggage. This exercise helps us see beyond them. The most important advice for this exercise is: take your time and be thorough. The temptation to rush is a facet of the mindset you're trying to avoid.

→ Working on your goal

As before, write down your ten next available goal times.

Goal calendar (preview)			
1 Date & time		Number of blocks	
2 Date & time		Number of blocks	
3 Date & time		Number of blocks	
4 Date & time		Number of blocks	
5 Date & time		Number of blocks	
6 Date & time		Number of blocks	
7 Date & time		Number of blocks	
8 Date & time		Number of blocks	
9 Date & time		Number of blocks	
10 Date & time		Number of blocks	

Leave the 'Number of blocks' field blank if not applicable.

Using your smartphone or online calendar, set an audible alarm for each of these times. (Please do not skip this step! This advice is repeated in every chapter.)

HOW TO TAKE ACTION

As before, use the BET questionnaire to record your experience. This time, should your motivation weaken, practise the exercises as directed.

This process comes in three parts:

▶ **Part 1** describes how to start working on your goal.

▶ **Part 2** describes how to continue working on your goal.

▶ **Part 3** describes how to take – and return from – your breaks.

Our aim is to follow the four simple rules of valuing time:

1 Start when you're supposed to start.

2 Divide your time into 'action blocks' where necessary.

3 Work on your goal without distraction.

4 Take regular breaks promptly.

If you struggle for motivation at any point, recognize that moment as a demotivating challenge. These exercises will help:

▶ Start by overriding demotivating challenges (Exercise 18).

▶ Follow this with tactical breathing (Exercise 19).

▶ If confused, check your 'next action' list. Is the next step clear?

▶ Try 'Reversing a negative mindset' (Exercise 31) if you recognize the thoughts discussed in this chapter.

▶ Finally, take action (Exercise 21) to focus on your goal.

Then continue with the next step, according to the exercise below.

Exercise 32

CONTINUING TO WORK ON YOUR GOAL

This exercise takes 45–50 minutes (plus stoppages) each time. It encourages you to work on your goal and record any demotivated periods. Complete the exercise every time you attempt an 'action block'.

Part 1: starting on time

Try to start promptly; be where you need to be and have everything you need. Write the date and time, and the task you're working on next, on a new BET record (see below).

If you started late, consider the thoughts, feelings, habits and behaviour that stood in your way. Answer the questionnaire below, using Part 1 of your current BET record.

Now set a 45-minute timer and get off to a good start by completing the following steps. Take two minutes or so to do the following.

→ Read your compelling vision statement.

→ Read your goal statement.

→ Read your action plan: which task(s) should you work on next?

→ Do Exercise 19, Tactical breathing.

→ Do Exercise 20, Tuning into the challenge.

→ Do Exercise 28, Planning your next actions.

→ Do Exercise 21, Taking action.

Part 2: working on my goal

Start working on your goal – without distraction – for the remainder of your action block. If your resolve weakens, recognize this moment as a demotivating challenge. Use the exercises listed above to ease past it.

Should you lose motivation for more than 60 seconds, answer the questionnaire below – this time using Part 2 of your current BET record. This information will prove invaluable. Then refocus on your goal.

Part 3: taking prompt breaks

After 45 minutes, start a 15-minute timer and take your break immediately. Leave your work area and focus on something else for a spell. Let your mind cool down!

Return from your break after 15 minutes and be ready to start your next action block, if scheduled.

Again, recognize the temptation to skip breaks (or return from them late) as demotivating challenges; combat such moments using the exercises above. If you become demotivated around your breaks, complete Part 3 of your BET record using the questionnaire below.

→ If you intend to carry on working, start a new 45-minute timer and follow the steps above. Use a new BET record each time, and repeat the exercises as requested. Should you complete four continuous action blocks, take a longer 45-minute break.

→ When you have finished, complete the quick review (Exercise 22). It takes only a couple of minutes. Treat any reluctance as another demotivating challenge. Use your new techniques to ease past it.

Follow the steps carefully and it will all make sense. If you can start an action block now, then do so. Otherwise, come back to this page when your next goal time starts.

Here's the questionnaire to use if you grind to a halt.

BET questionnaire	
1	What **behaviour** did you do instead of working on your goal?
2	What **emotions** did you feel about working on your goal?
3	What **thoughts** discouraged you? Did you excuse yourself from taking action? Did you think negatively about the task ahead?
4	Was any of this **habitual**? (Did you distract yourself without consciously deciding to do so?)

Answering these questions takes moments. Be brief, but try to record some detail.

What to do next

Take a moment to complete these exercises and refocus on your goal:

1 Start by overriding demotivating challenges (Exercise 18).

2 Follow this with tactical breathing (Exercise 19).

3 Finally, take action (Exercise 21) to focus on your goal.

These techniques should get you moving again.

As before, use the following form to record your answers to the questions.

BET record

Date:

Task:

Part 1: starting on time

Behaviour:
Emotions:
Thoughts:
Habit (Y/N):

Part 2: working on my goal

During: 1   2   3
Behaviour:
Emotions:
Thoughts:
Habit (Y/N):

During: 4   5   6
Behaviour:
Emotions:
Thoughts:
Habit (Y/N):

Part 3: taking prompt breaks

Start of break:
Behaviour:
Emotions:
Thoughts:
Habit (Y/N):

End of break:
Behaviour:
Emotions:
Thoughts:
Habit (Y/N):

Keep your notes brief, but remember that tracking these distractions will help.

POINTS TO REMEMBER

Use Exercise 32 to guide you, and attempt the techniques as frequently as possible. Try not to skip them; you are building powerful new habits.

Use the questionnaire to make notes whenever your motivation falters.

▸ Use a new BET record for each action block you attempt. This data will prove invaluable.

▸ Complete at least ten BET records before moving on to the next chapter.

▶ Ideally, complete the ten BET records across a number of sittings (your findings will then be more representative).

This process should now be starting to feel familiar. Soon, it will become second nature.

→ Demotivating challenges

Pay extra attention to your thoughts and feelings. If you recognize the mindsets discussed earlier in this chapter, the 'Reversing a negative mindset' exercise will help (particularly when used in conjunction with the tactical breathing exercise from Chapter 8).

Gently guide yourself towards your best interests. Have your motivation fact sheet to hand, and use the various techniques to stay on track.

Here is the list of the various challenges you may face.

Challenges		
Demotivating behaviour	Demotivating emotions	Demotivating thoughts
Any activity other than working towards your goal	*Complacency:* ignoring the importance of working towards your goal, e.g. 'I can't be bothered', or 'It's not important.'	*Plausible excuses:* thoughts that give you permission to focus elsewhere, despite not standing up to scrutiny, e.g. 'I don't have to do this yet', or 'I don't have everything I need.'
Over-planning: excessively planning action instead of taking action	*Reluctance, tiredness, boredom, frustration, anxiety, and feeling overwhelmed:* abandoning your commitment to your goal	*Value judgements:* your appraisal of the tasks ahead, e.g. 'It's boring', or 'It's not going to be good enough'.
General dithering: present but not really doing anything	*Despondency:* a sense that you cannot do it	
Daydreaming: staring into space, wishing to be elsewhere or thinking that your goal is complete	*Temptation:* wanting to abandon your goal for something more interesting	
Habitual avoidance: switching focus elsewhere without consciously thinking about it	*Compulsive avoidance:* feeling unable to work on your goal, and yet also feeling bad, guilty, stressed or 'stuck'	

Summary

Irrational and negative mindsets have a huge impact on our lives. Use the exercises from this chapter whenever you need to. They will help you see more clearly and give you the freedom to act at will.

Remember to relax, and see limiting mindsets for what they really are: a persistent illusion. Complete at least ten BET records before moving on to the next chapter.

What I have learned

→ What are my thoughts, feelings and insights on what I have read so far?

_____

_____

_____

Use the space below to summarize any actions you identify as a result of reading this chapter.

_____

_____

_____

_____

Where to next?

In the next chapter we will explore ways to overcome both unhelpful habits and the temptation to make excuses for our lack of self-motivation. Bring these under control and your motivation will increase significantly. Until then, work on your goal and do your best to stay on track.

12 Overcoming unhelpful habits and excuses

In this chapter:

▶ you will learn about habits, and how they destroy motivation
▶ you will identify your 'demotivating excuses' and discover how they run contrary to your best interests
▶ you will discover a simple technique to eradicate compulsive distraction that will, with practice, increase your motivation dramatically.

Despite everything you have practised so far, you may still find yourself becoming easily distracted. Bad habits and excuses can destroy motivation in a split second, so we need to bring them under control. As always, this means building greater awareness.

Habits are an efficient way of doing things, so our mind seeks constantly to create them. Because we deploy them without much thought, we are free to focus elsewhere. Life would be tiring and dangerous otherwise. However, this process can go wrong if a habit compels us to act against our best interests. Similarly, seeking refuge in demotivating excuses, even if they seem plausible at the time, destroys motivation and is extremely destructive.

→ The habitual mind

Habits have cropped up frequently throughout this workbook. In Chapter 3 we discussed the 'habitual mind'. This part of us automates repeated thoughts and behaviours.

Habits come in all shapes and sizes. Do you recognize any of the following?

▶ Pressing the snooze button twice before getting out of bed

▶ Making the bed each morning

▶ Checking your emails as soon as you arrive at work

▶ Feeling the need for a cup of coffee at certain times of the day

▶ Choosing the same lunch without considering the alternatives

▶ Switching the TV on at the same time of day

▶ Checking the fridge when you arrive home

▶ Following the same evening routine before bed

Any repeated thought or behaviour can turn into a habit. This causes problems if the habit is particularly destructive. We are compelled to act, even at the expense of our best interests. Habits are powerful because they override our control.

'The gods help them that help themselves.'

Aesop

HOW DO HABITS WORK?

Habits unfold in three simple steps:

1 **The cue**

   This can be anything – from certain times or places, thoughts or feelings, to external events or people.

2 **The routine**

   This is a sequence of steps 'chunked' together so that they flow from one to the next.

3 **The reward**

   This is the 'end state' that lets the habitual mind know that everything has gone according to *its* plan (although sometimes not *our* plan).

How does this look in real life? One simple example is the 'making a cup of tea' habit:

▶ **Cue:** You realize you are thirsty (or perhaps bored).

▶ **Routine:** You stop what you are doing, walk to the kettle, fill it and switch it on; select a cup and add the teabag; add the hot water, milk and sugar according to taste; let it brew a little, stir, and dispose of the teabag.

▶ **Reward:** You now have a cup of tea.

These 12 steps unfold without much conscious input. Even delicate moments can be carried out without great concentration. (Have you ever poured too much milk because your mind was elsewhere? This author shares your dismay.)

Hundreds of habits are deployed each day. Life would be very taxing otherwise. Notice how this habit could be cued by *boredom*. The relationship between 'cue' and 'habit' is just simple association. This is not always helpful, as we shall see.

William's story

William, a young architecture student from Devon, was really enjoying university. However, he knew it was time to knuckle down. He dreamed of becoming an architect, and recognized that he had just one chance of turning his dream into reality.

William started doing everything *by the book*. He created a compelling vision statement and a SMART goal; he drew up his action plan and identified his goal time. He worked in action blocks, and used various techniques to stay on track. William's approached could not be faulted.

Despite this, he still found himself constantly distracted. Sometimes he managed to control it, but often he spiralled into despair. Hours could easily be lost. With mounting frustration, he reviewed his BET records for clues.

William's problem lay with certain bad habits. Here are a few examples.

The 'Facebook' habit

▶ Cue: each time William switched his laptop on

▶ Routine: he automatically logged into Facebook

▶ Reward: Facebook was open and all was 'well'.

William's urge to 'first check my Facebook' frustrated him massively. This habit had been established over several years. Although it severely hampered his focus, the habitual mind does not evaluate such things. Habits are compelling and resisting this habit would feel uncomfortable, despite being the rational thing to do. Habits can be destructive because they are unthinking.

The 'putting things off until tomorrow' habit

- ▸ Cue: each time William felt stressed about his assignments
- ▸ Routine: the thought 'I'll start it in a bit' flashed through his mind and guided his focus elsewhere
- ▸ Reward: the avoidance of stress – the habitual brain has succeeded in its aim.

William's repeated avoidance of stress had become entrenched. Whenever he felt stressed, this habit automatically directed his focus elsewhere. He then struggled to feel in control.

The 'last minute' habit

- ▸ Cue: whenever William considered a deadline
- ▸ Routine: he quickly calculated how long he had until 'the last minute'
- ▸ Reward: he could now wait as long as possible before swinging into action.

William had always left things until the last minute. Now, whenever considering time or deadlines, his habitual mind took over. Without paying much attention, William habitually calculated how long he could wait before acting. This habit interfered with everything, from meeting friends to completing important assignments.

→ Habitual avoidance and distraction

The problem should be clear from the above examples: demotivating habits are quick, semi-conscious and pervasive – and they force us to act against our best interests. To make the most of our time, demotivating habits must be overcome.

Let's review your completed BET records for clues. You're looking for *automatic* demotivating thoughts or behaviours, those moments where you delayed or switched focus without realizing it.

IDENTIFYING BAD HABITS

This exercise takes just a few minutes. The aim of the exercise is to identify habitual demotivation.

1 Read through the BET records completed so far. Look out for times when you:

▶ started late without really thinking about it

▶ became distracted without really thinking about it

▶ took your break late without really thinking about it

▶ returned from your break without really thinking about it.

Pay attention to moments where you noted 'N/A' for thoughts or emotions. This indicates a demotivating habit.

2 Read through the following checklist and tick anything that rings true.

Demotivating habits sometimes mean that:

I do not start on time.	☐
I become distracted while working.	☐
I do not take breaks at the right time.	☐
I do not return from breaks on time.	☐

Habits are easy to break, providing you catch them in time. We will explore that shortly. Before moving on, you'll need to update your motivation fact sheet.

Exercise 34

ADDING TO YOUR MOTIVATION FACT SHEET

This exercise takes just a few minutes. It updates your motivation fact sheet.

1 On the document you created entitled 'Motivation fact sheet', create a new sub-heading: 'I need to look out for these bad habits'.

2 Then list the demotivating habits you identified above.

Motivation fact sheet (example)	
I sometimes struggle with motivation because	*I do not start on time.* *I become distracted.* *I do not take my breaks on time* *I do not return from breaks on time.*
I need to avoid these behaviours	*Logging on to social networking sites* *Checking my email* *Making snacks* *Texting or calling friends*
When starting, I need to look out for these emotions	*Complacency*
When working, I need to look out for these emotions	*Reluctance, tiredness, boredom and despondency* *Frustration and anxiety*
When restarting after a break, I should be wary of these emotions	*Complacency* *The temptation to do other things*
I need to look out for these bad habits	*I become distracted while working.* *I do not take breaks at the right time.*

Keep your fact-sheet document visible if possible. If necessary, email yourself a copy to view on your smartphone.

→ Demotivating excuses

The human mind is complicated. Our beliefs, desires, values, and fears often come into conflict. This is known as cognitive dissonance – and it plays an important role in motivation. For example, imagine somebody who wants to lose weight but struggles to control their 'comfort eating'. Logically they know that losing weight would improve their confidence. Unfortunately, they comfort eat to ease negative feelings. Viewed rationally, this short-term fix only makes things worse. However, comfort eating is an emotional behaviour; logic plays little part in it.

Essentially, in situations like this we are caught in two minds. The conflict creates unpleasant tension, so we search for a get-out clause:

▶ 'It's okay, I'll be really good tomorrow and make up for it.'

▶ 'I've already decided now. I'll get back to healthy eating tomorrow.'

▶ 'I've already stuffed myself – what's the point in stopping now?'

▶ 'That dessert looks far too nice to pass over! Just this once...'

These thoughts, known as 'demotivating excuses', are extremely destructive.

YOUR PRIVATE INNER WORLD

Thinking is constant and involuntary, with one thought flowing into the next. People think in a variety of ways. For example, our inner voice chatters away while images and memories flash through our minds. Sometimes thoughts seem more like emotions. Our understanding is derived from gut feelings and bodily sensations.

Either way, stopping yourself from thinking is difficult. Our minds are rarely still – even when we are asleep – and yet we often pay little attention to our thoughts. This is a problem, particularly where demotivating excuses are concerned. These excuses may be categorized into several types:

▶ **Auditory excuses**

We use our inner voice to state excuses, e.g. 'It's okay to do this later' or 'I can't do this yet – I don't have everything I need.'

▶ **Visual excuses**

Sometimes we visualize our excuses – creating mental images of 'reasons' to delay or temping alternative activities.

▶ **Emotional excuses**

We also feel our excuses. We 'know' we have excused ourselves from action because we feel a sense of relief.

▶ **Habitual excuses**

As we saw earlier, repetitive thoughts become habits. Over time, our excuses become automatic, lightning-fast and difficult to control.

▶ **Combined excuses**

Sometimes the mind combines our inner voice, visual imagery and emotional impulses to powerful effect.

Demotivating excuses seem plausible, and they often contain some truth. However, they are *just* thoughts. We may feel keen to accept them, but in reality they ruin lives. Dismissing excuses is paramount, because you're then more likely to stay in control.

Excuses tend to fall into three broad categories:

▶ 'I can't do this yet, because...'

▶ 'I don't have to do this yet, because...'

▶ 'It's okay to do this other thing first.'

Consider the list in the next exercise and see how many excuses you identify with.

RECOGNIZING DEMOTIVATING EXCUSES

This exercise takes just a few minutes. It identifies the demotivating excuses you use to avoid working on your goal.

▶ Read through the following list and tick any excuses that seem familiar.

▶ Remember, our excuses can be thought using our *inner voice*, through *mental imagery* or via our *emotional understanding*.

▶ There is space for your own examples if required.

Impossibility

I don't have the motivation to do this right now. ☐

I haven't got enough time; I'll start when... ☐

I'm too busy to do this now because... ☐

I'll do it in a bit. ☐

I'm too tired to do this now; I'll start it later. ☐

I'm too stressed to do this now; I'll start later. ☐

I don't know what to do next; I'll have a break and come back to it. ☐

I don't know where to start; I'll have a break and come back to it. ☐

I haven't got everything I need; I'll start when... ☐

→ Write your own examples here:

1 _____

2 _____

3 _____

4 _____

Non-obligatory

I'll do it tomorrow! ☐

I don't need to do this yet, because... ☐

It's not a priority right now. ☐

I just can't be bothered! ☐

I work best when I'm under pressure – I'll wait, for now. ☐

It will all be fine! ☐

Doing this now will make no difference anyway. ☐

→ Write your own examples here:

1 _____

2 _____

3 _____

4 _____

Tempting alternatives

Just five more minutes! ☐

I will do it, but I'll just do this other thing first... ☐

If I leave it now, he or she will do it instead. ☐

I'll leave this for now, but I promise I'll make up for it later. ☐

I want to do this other thing instead... ☐

It's not as important as this other thing; I'll do it later... ☐

→ Write your own examples here:

1 _____

2 _____

3 _____

4 _____

Ultimately, these excuses are seductive lies. No matter how plausible they seem, their only purpose is to relieve stress. Your emotional mind might want to avoid something, but succumbing to these excuses will only hold you back.

Have you noticed how we keep our excuses private? We know they don't stand up to scrutiny, and we'd feel far too embarrassed to share them. Our friends would see right through them, which tells you everything you need to know.

 Exercise 36

ADDING TO YOUR MOTIVATION FACT SHEET

This exercise takes just a few minutes. It updates your motivation fact sheet.

1 On the document you created entitled 'Motivation fact sheet', create a new sub-heading: 'I need to look out for these demotivating excuses'.

2 Then list the demotivating excuses you identified above.

Motivation fact sheet (example)	
I sometimes struggle with motivation because	*I do not start on time.* *I become distracted.* *I do not take my breaks on time* *I do not return from breaks on time.*
I need to avoid these behaviours	*Logging on to social networking sites* *Checking my email* *Making snacks* *Texting or calling friends*
When starting, I need to look out for these emotions	*Complacency*
When working, I need to look out for these emotions	*Reluctance, tiredness, boredom and despondency* *Frustration and anxiety*
When restarting after a break, I should be wary of these emotions	*Complacency* *The temptation to do other things*
I need to look out for these bad habits	*I become distracted while working.* *I do not take breaks at the right time.*
I need to look out for these demotivating excuses	*I will do it, but I'll just do this other thing first.* *I'll do it in a bit.* *I'm too tired to do this now; I'll start it later.* *I'm too stressed to do this now; I'll start later.*

Again, keep your fact-sheet document visible if possible and refer to it often.

→ Ideas into practice

You can now put these ideas to the test. A new technique to try is the 'Dismissing bad habits and excuses' exercise below. Use it whenever you find yourself acting against your best interests without your conscious thought. It takes just seconds to do, so use it as frequently as possible.

To build your skills, keep practising the exercises introduced in previous chapters:

► overriding demotivating challenges (Exercise 18).

► tactical breathing (Exercise 19)

► reversing a negative mindset (Exercise 31)

► tuning into the challenge (Exercise 20)

► planning your next actions (Exercise 28)

► taking action (Exercise 21)

► quick review (Exercise 22).

If your motivation weakens, use these techniques to get back on track. You do not need to give in to every demotivating challenge.

Look out for the bad habits and demotivating excuses discussed in this chapter. The following exercise will help, and it takes just moments. Used repeatedly, it forms a *positive* habit – and you'll regain your sense of control.

 **Exercise 37**

DISMISSING BAD HABITS AND EXCUSES

This exercise takes just seconds. It restores self-control by dismissing bad habits and excuses. Use it whenever you are: a) about to distract yourself; b) distracting yourself; or c) have just distracted yourself.

 1 Are you experiencing the urge to focus elsewhere? Acknowledge this and state: 'That's just a bad habit created by my brain.' Grasp the reality; there is more to you than this impulse.

2 Did you excuse yourself from working on your goal? Look out for:

➜ 'I can't do this, because...'

➜ 'I don't have to do this yet, because...'

➜ 'It's okay to do this other thing first.'

If you are unsure, ask yourself: 'How am I excusing this distraction?' Acknowledge the excuse and affirm: 'That's just an excuse created by my brain.'

3 Ideally, catch yourself before switching away from your goal. Pause for five seconds, breathe slowly and relax. If possible and appropriate, sit on your hands – for some reason, this helps! If you've already switched away from your goal, don't worry. Use these steps as soon as you notice. You'll improve with greater awareness and practice.

4 Remember: you do not need to give in to these challenges. Focus on what you *can* do, and switch back to your goal.

Demotivating habits and excuses rob us of our *self-control*. This exercise injects some reality into the situation. Complete these steps and put yourself back in the driving seat.

Pausing for the whole five seconds is important. This interferes with unhelpful unconscious processes. Intervene whenever you notice your focus is shifting. With practice, you'll be able to nip distractions in the bud.

Sometimes this technique causes frustration. If so, use the tactical breathing exercise from Chapter 8. These two exercises, when used in conjunction, will dramatically improve your concentration.

→ Working on your goal

As before, write down your ten next available goal times.

Goal calendar (preview)			
1 Date & time		Number of blocks	
2 Date & time		Number of blocks	
3 Date & time		Number of blocks	
4 Date & time		Number of blocks	
5 Date & time		Number of blocks	
6 Date & time		Number of blocks	
7 Date & time		Number of blocks	
8 Date & time		Number of blocks	
9 Date & time		Number of blocks	
10 Date & time		Number of blocks	

Leave the 'Number of blocks' field blank if not applicable. Then, using your smartphone or online calendar, set an audible alarm for each of these times. (Please do not skip this step! This advice is repeated in every chapter.)

HOW TO TAKE ACTION

As before, use the BET questionnaire to record your experience. Practise the exercises whenever you need to.

This process comes in three parts:

▶ **Part 1** describes how to start working on your goal.

▶ **Part 2** describes how to continue working on your goal.

▶ **Part 3** describes how to take – and return from – your breaks.

Our aim is to follow the four simple rules of valuing time:

1 Start when you're supposed to start.

2 Divide your time into 'action blocks' where necessary.

3 Work on your goal without distraction.

4 Take regular breaks promptly.

If you struggle for motivation at any point, recognize that moment as a demotivating challenge.

▶ Use 'Dismissing bad habits and excuses' (Exercise 37) to combat habitual distraction and demotivating excuses.

▶ Use 'Overriding demotivating challenges' (Exercise 18) when demotivation feels more compelling.

▶ Follow this with tactical breathing (Exercise 19).

▶ If confused, check your 'next action' list. Is the next step clear?

▶ Try 'Reversing a negative mindset' (Exercise 31) if you recognize the thoughts discussed in Chapter 11.

▶ Finally, take action (Exercise 21) to focus on your goal.

Then continue with the next step, according to the exercise below.

 *Exercise 38*

WORKING ON YOUR GOAL

This exercise takes 45–50 minutes (plus stoppages) each time. It encourages you to work on your goal and record any demotivated periods. Complete the exercise every time you attempt an 'action block'.

Part 1: starting on time

Try to start promptly; be where you need to be and have everything you need. Write the date and time, and the task you're working on next, on a new BET record (see below).

If you started late, consider the thoughts, feelings, habits and behaviour that stood in your way. Answer the questionnaire below, using Part 1 of your current BET record.

Now set a 45-minute timer and get off to a good start by completing the following steps. Take two minutes or so to do the following.

→ Read your compelling vision statement.

→ Read your goal statement.

→ Read your action plan: which task(s) should you work on next?

→ Complete Exercise 19, Tactical breathing.

→ Complete Exercise 20, Tuning into the challenge.

→ Complete Exercise 28, Planning your next actions.

→ Complete Exercise 21, Taking action.

Part 2: working on my goal

Start working on your goal – without distraction – for the remainder of your action block. If your resolve weakens, recognize this as a demotivating challenge. Use the exercises listed above to ease past it.

Should you lose motivation for more than 60 seconds, answer the questionnaire below – this time using Part 2 of your current BET record. This information will prove invaluable. Then refocus on your goal.

Part 3: taking prompt breaks

After 45 minutes, start a 15-minute timer and take your break immediately. Leave your work area and focus on something else for a spell. Let your mind cool down!

Return from your break after 15 minutes and be ready to start your next action block, if scheduled.

Again, recognize the temptation to skip breaks (or return from them late) as demotivating challenges; combat such moments using the exercises above. If you become demotivated around your breaks, complete Part 3 of your BET record using the questionnaire below.

→ If you intend to carry on working, start a new 45-minute timer and follow the steps above. Use a new BET record each time, and repeat the exercises as requested. Should you complete four continuous action blocks, take a longer 45-minute break.

→ When you have finished, complete the quick review (Exercise 22). It takes only a couple of minutes. Treat any reluctance as another demotivating challenge. Use your new techniques to ease past it.

Follow the steps carefully and it will all make sense. If you can start an action block now, then do so. Otherwise, come back to this page when your next goal time starts.

Here's the questionnaire to use if you grind to a halt.

BET questionnaire	
1	What **behaviour** did you do instead of working on your goal?
2	What **emotions** did you feel about working on your goal?
3	What **thoughts** discouraged you? Did you excuse yourself from taking action? Did you think negatively about the task ahead?
4	Was any of this **habitual**? (Did you distract yourself without consciously deciding to do so?)

Answering these questions takes moments. Be brief, but try to record some detail.

What to do next

Take a moment to complete these exercises and refocus on your goal:

1 Start by overriding demotivating challenges (Exercise 18).

2 Follow this with tactical breathing (Exercise 19).

3 Finally, take action (Exercise 21) to focus on your goal.

These techniques should get you moving again.

Use the BET record form to record your answers to the questions.

BET record

Date:

Task:

Part 1: starting on time

Behaviour:
Emotions:
Thoughts:
Habit (Y/N):

Part 2: working on my goal

During:	1	2	3
Behaviour:			
Emotions:			
Thoughts:			
Habit (Y/N):			

During:	4	5	6
Behaviour:			
Emotions:			
Thoughts:			
Habit (Y/N):			

Part 3: taking prompt breaks

Start of break:	**End of break:**
Behaviour:	Behaviour:
Emotions:	Emotions:
Thoughts:	Thoughts:
Habit (Y/N):	Habit (Y/N):

Keep your notes brief, but clearly identify the thoughts, feelings, habits and behaviours that are behind any demotivating challenges. Tracking these distractions always helps.

POINTS TO REMEMBER

Use the 'Working on your goal' exercise to guide you, and attempt the techniques as frequently as possible. Try not to skip any of them; you are building powerful new habits.

Use the questionnaire to make notes whenever your motivation falters:

▶ Use a new BET record for each action block you attempt. This data will prove invaluable.

▶ Complete at least ten BET records before moving on to the next chapter.

▶ Ideally, complete the ten BET records across a number of sittings (your findings will then be more representative).

This process should now be starting to feel familiar. Soon, it will become second nature.

→ Demotivating challenges

Keep your motivation fact sheet to hand. When you are tempted to switch away from your goal, use the 'Dismissing bad habits and excuses' exercise to catch yourself (followed by the tactical breathing exercise if you feel stressed).

In the meantime, keep gently guiding yourself towards your best interests. Use the exercises introduced so far to stay on track.

Summary

The techniques in this chapter are simple. Use them to dismiss destructive habits and excuses before they take hold. With just a little practice, your concentration and focus will increase dramatically. In this way you will be able to dismiss bad habits and excuses quickly. And remember to relax.

Complete at least ten BET records before moving on to the next chapter.

What I have learned

→ What are my thoughts, feelings and insights on what I have read so far?

_____

_____

_____

Use the space below to summarize any actions you identify as a result of reading this chapter.

_____

_____

_____

_____

Where to next?

We've now learned more about the demotivating challenges we face, and discovered techniques to overcome them. In the next chapter we will turn our attention to the art of feeling motivated in the moment. With practice, you will learn to feel motivated at will.

13 The art of feeling motivated

▶ you will discover the power of desire and learn how to use it

▶ you will explore a technique for creating desire in the present moment

▶ you will learn how to amplify motivated feelings at will.

Your work so far has focused on overcoming demotivating challenges. These moments are created by unruly signals in your brain. The resulting thoughts and feelings seem real enough, but this constricted state of consciousness is a damaging illusion. It needlessly deters us from our best interests.

Step beyond such moments and your motivation naturally increases. It then depends on a simple question: is the effort worth the reward? As we saw in Chapter 8, this question can still pose problems. Future rewards are too easily discounted. This often results in a feeling of complacency, and our motivation subsequently falters.

> *'Either life entails courage, or it ceases to be life.'*
>
> E. M. Forster

→ Action is the goal

Building strong motivation means accomplishing three simple aims:

▶ Step beyond demotivating challenges.

▶ Connect with your desire to achieve your goal.

▶ Recognize that your action plan and your goal are the same thing.

Desiring the goal means that you must desire the action – even if you cannot feel it. And this is the very nub of motivation: judging upcoming action so that it provokes willingness, eagerness and necessity of movement – because we desire the result. It might seem obvious, but people easily forget this.

In Chapter 10, you learned techniques to help you keep things in perspective. Motivation increases or decreases depending on our thoughts about forthcoming tasks, and your motivation will be strong providing you desire the outcome *and* keep the task in perspective. Achieve this repeatedly and you'll achieve your goals. It can be straightforward if you recognize any lack of desire as just another illusion to overcome: a simple quirk of consciousness. Instead, resolve to make an effort. Your results then reflect the work you put in.

Of course, this is always easier if you can really feel desire. Let's explore two powerful techniques to get you moving.

> '*People often say that motivation doesn't last. Well, neither does bathing. That's why we recommend it daily.*'
>
> Zig Ziglar

→ Ideas into action

You can now put these ideas to the test when you return to work on your goal once more.

In this chapter, we'll practise linking desire to your 'next actions'. Two new techniques to try are:

- ▶ energizing your emotional mind (Exercise 39)
- ▶ spinning motivated feelings (Exercise 40).

These exercises work mostly with emotion. They foster greater desire and willingness, as you shall see.

In addition, continue practising the exercises introduced in previous chapters:

- ▶ overriding demotivating challenges (Exercise 18).
- ▶ tactical breathing (Exercise 19)
- ▶ reversing a negative mindset (Exercise 31)
- ▶ dismissing habits and excuses (Exercise 37)
- ▶ tuning into the challenge (Exercise 20).

- planning your next actions (Exercise 28)
- taking action (Exercise 21)
- quick review (Exercise 22).

If your motivation weakens, use these techniques to get back on track. You do not need to give in to every demotivating challenge.

ENERGIZING YOUR EMOTIONAL MIND

This exercise takes just seconds. It fires up your desire and willingness to act, making action more likely. Use it whenever you want to take sustained positive action.

1 Feeling motivated means holding a desire and willingness to act. To fire that up, scan through your compelling vision statement. Pick out the *words and ideas* that stoke your inner desire. Tell yourself: 'It's okay to want this!'

2 Next, close your eyes and spend 60 seconds mentally 'acting out' achieving your goal. Focus on the ideas and feelings you picked out in step 1. Imagine it vividly; get your emotions going.

Visualizing works by suspending your disbelief and 'pretending' that what you desire is really happening. You don't need clear mental imagery; just *act it out* in your mind. This should create relatively strong feelings.

3 Link the future with the present. Keeping the desire in your body, close your eyes and imagine completing your 'next actions'. Incorporate everything you have learned so far: relaxed action, a clear mindset, dismissing excuses, etc. Understand this: desiring this goal means you *must* desire the next action – even if you cannot sense it (yet).

Recognize that your action and your goal are the same thing. Taking action meets your needs, expresses your values and achieves your compelling vision. Your goal and your action plan are *cut from the same cloth*.

Following these steps links positive feelings to the tasks immediately ahead of you. This should create a desire and willingness to act.

The next exercise amplifies positive emotions. It requires some practice at first, but it will make a huge difference to your motivation levels. Give it a try now.

SPINNING MOTIVATED FEELINGS

This exercise takes five minutes to learn, and a minute or so to use; practise it often. It amplifies positive feelings in the body, so use it whenever you need to boost your motivation. Read through the steps first and familiarize yourself with them.

1 Focus on your 'next action' now. Think about enjoying the rewards. Vividly imagine your circumstances improving, and feel desire.

2 Observe the feelings in your body, and answer the following questions:

→ What is the location of the desire in my body (stomach, chest, face, cheeks, shoulders, etc.)?

_____

→ How does the feeling move? Is it a rising or a sinking feeling? Is it a tight knot? Does it spin clockwise or anticlockwise? (Feelings move through the body; they pulse, shoot, spin and fizz around. Take a moment to identify these movements.)

_____

→ Does the feeling move quickly or slowly?

_____

→ What texture does it have – smooth, fuzzy, rough, tingly, spiky, no texture?

_____

→ Is it narrow or wide? Is it hotter or colder than the rest of your body?

_____

→ How intense is this feeling, on a scale of one to ten?

_____

→ If the feeling had a colour, what would it be? (Just guess!)

_____

You may need to carry out these steps several times to answer the questions fully.

 3 Once you have a handle on the feeling, imagine you can reach into it and push it strongly through your body. Each time you inhale, attempt the following:

→ Imagine growing more determined and motivated.

→ Imagine the feeling moving with greater depth and power.

→ Imagine the feeling growing wider and more intense.

→ If the feeling is moving from your stomach to your chest (for example), push it up and beyond, into your shoulders and your face.

→ Make the 'colour' brighter and more vibrant.

Spend a minute or so moving the motivated feeling around your body. If you lose focus, recall the rewards associated with your goal and reconnect with your desire. Spin it around and amplify it.

When using this technique, it is useful to imagine scooping up handfuls of water and creating powerful waves. Making the waves stronger amplifies the feelings. Practise this as often as possible; it makes a huge difference.

→ Working on your goal

As before, write down your ten next available goal times.

Goal calendar (preview)			
1 Date & time		Number of blocks	
2 Date & time		Number of blocks	
3 Date & time		Number of blocks	
4 Date & time		Number of blocks	
5 Date & time		Number of blocks	
6 Date & time		Number of blocks	
7 Date & time		Number of blocks	
8 Date & time		Number of blocks	
9 Date & time		Number of blocks	
10 Date & time		Number of blocks	

Leave the 'Number of blocks' field blank if not applicable.

Using your smartphone or online calendar, set an audible alarm for each of these times. (Please do not skip this step! This advice is repeated in every chapter.)

HOW TO TAKE ACTION

As before, use the BET questionnaire to record your experience. Practise the exercises whenever your motivation weakens.

This process comes in three parts:

▶ **Part 1** describes how to start working on your goal.

▶ **Part 2** describes how to continue working on your goal.

▶ **Part 3** describes how to take – and return from – your breaks.

Our aim is to follow the four simple rules of valuing time:

1 Start when you're supposed to start.

2 Divide your time into 'action blocks' where necessary.

3 Work on your goal without distraction.

4 Take regular breaks promptly.

At any stage – before starting, while working on your goal, before taking a break, when returning from a break – you may struggle to motivate yourself. Recognize these moments as demotivating challenges and try to work through them. The next exercise explains how.

If you struggle for motivation at any point, recognize that moment as a demotivating challenge

▶ Use 'Dismissing bad habits and excuses' (Exercise 37) to combat habitual distraction and demotivating excuses.

▶ Use 'Overriding demotivating challenges' (Exercise 18) when demotivation feels more compelling.

▶ Follow this with tactical breathing (Exercise 19).

▶ If confused, check your 'next action' list. Is the next step clear?

▶ Try 'Reversing a negative mindset' (Exercise 31) if you recognize the thoughts discussed in Chapter 11.

▶ Finally, take action (Exercise 21) to focus on your goal.

Then continue with the next step, according to the exercise below.

WORKING ON THE GOAL

This exercise takes 45–50 minutes (plus stoppages) each time. It encourages you to work on your goal and record any demotivated periods. Complete the exercise every time you attempt an 'action block'.

Part 1: starting on time

Try to start promptly; be where you need to be and have everything you need. Write the date and time, and the task you're working on next, on a new BET record (see below).

If you started late, consider the thoughts, feelings, habits and behaviour that stood in your way. Answer the questionnaire below, using Part 1 of your current BET record.

Now set a 45-minute timer and get off to a good start by completing the following steps. Take two minutes or so to do the following.

→ Read your compelling vision statement.

→ Read your goal statement.

→ Read your action plan: which task(s) should you work on next?

→ Complete Exercise 19, Tactical breathing.

→ Complete Exercise 20, Tuning into the challenge.

→ Complete Exercise 28, Planning your next actions.

→ Complete Exercise 39, Energizing your emotional mind.

→ Complete Exercise 21, Taking action.

Part 2: working on my goal

Start working on your goal – without distraction – for the remainder of your action block. If your resolve weakens, recognize this as a demotivating challenge. Use the exercises practised so far to ease past it.

Should you lose motivation for more than 60 seconds, answer the questionnaire below – this time using Part 2 of your current BET record. This information will prove invaluable. Then refocus on your goal.

Part 3: taking prompt breaks

After 45 minutes, start a 15-minute timer and take your break immediately. Leave your work area and focus on something else for a spell. Let your mind cool down!

Return from your break after 15 minutes and be ready to start your next action block, if scheduled.

Again, recognize the temptation to skip breaks (or return from them late) as demotivating challenges; combat such moments using the exercises above. If you become demotivated around your breaks, complete Part 3 of your BET record using the questionnaire below.

→ If you intend to carry on working, start a new 45-minute timer and follow the steps above. Use a new BET record each time, and repeat the exercises as requested. Should you complete four continuous action blocks, take a longer 45-minute break.

→ When you have finished, complete the quick review (Exercise 22). It takes only a couple of minutes. Treat any reluctance as another demotivating challenge. Use your new techniques to ease past it.

Follow the steps carefully and it will all make sense. If you can start an action block now, then do so. Otherwise, come back to this page when your next goal time starts.

Here's the questionnaire to use if you grind to a halt.

BET questionnaire
1   What **behaviour** did you do instead of working on your goal?
2   What **emotions** did you feel about working on your goal?
3   What **thoughts** discouraged you? Did you excuse yourself from taking action? Did you think negatively about the task ahead?
4   Was any of this **habitual**? (Did you distract yourself without consciously deciding to do so?)

Answering these questions takes moments. Be brief, but try to record some detail.

What to do next

Take a moment to complete these exercises and refocus on your goal:

1 Start by overriding demotivating challenges (Exercise 18).

2 Follow this with tactical breathing (Exercise 19).

3 Finally, take action (Exercise 21) to focus on your goal.

These techniques should get you moving again.

Once again, use the BET form to record your answers to the questions.

<u>BET record</u>

Date:

Task:

Part 1: starting on time

Behaviour:
Emotions:
Thoughts:
Habit (Y/N):

Part 2: working on my goal

During: 1	2	3
Behaviour:		
Emotions:		
Thoughts:		
Habit (Y/N):		

During: 4	5	6
Behaviour:		
Emotions:		
Thoughts:		
Habit (Y/N):		

Part 3: taking prompt breaks

Start of break:	**End of break:**
Behaviour:	Behaviour:
Emotions:	Emotions:
Thoughts:	Thoughts:
Habit (Y/N):	Habit (Y/N):

Keep your notes brief, but clearly identify the thoughts, feelings, habits and behaviours behind any demotivating challenges. Tracking these distractions continues to build motivation.

POINTS TO REMEMBER

Use the 'Working on your goal' exercise to guide you, and attempt the techniques as frequently as possible. Try not skip them; they are building powerful new habits.

Use the questionnaire to make notes whenever your motivation falters.

▶ Use a new BET record for each action block you attempt. This data will prove invaluable.

▶ Complete at least ten BET records before moving on to the next chapter.

▶ Ideally, complete the ten BET records across a number of sittings (your findings will then be more representative).

You'll now be starting to feel familiar with this process, but keep practising, and it will become second nature.

→ Demotivating challenges

Use the two exercises from this chapter to promote *desire*. See beyond the human illusion of discounted reward: your next actions and your goal are the same thing. The 'Spinning motivated feelings' exercise will boost your positive emotions.

Keep up the habit of gently guiding yourself towards your best interests. Use the various exercises to stay on track, and keep your motivation fact sheet to hand. (The full list of exercises for the motivation process is in Appendix 1 at the back of this workbook.)

Summary

In reality, you don't need to feel motivated to take action. However, the techniques introduced in this chapter do help. Understand the true nature of the tasks ahead of you: they are just little chunks of your goal. Grasping this fully aligns our emotional mind to our best interests. Remember to stoke up your desire!

Complete at least ten more BET records before moving on to the next chapter.

What I have learned

→ What are my thoughts, feelings and insights on what I have read so far?

_____

_____

_____

Use the space below to summarize any actions you identify as a result of reading this chapter.

_____

_____

_____

_____

Where to next?

In the next chapter we will return our attention to goal setting. For now, practise the exercises in this chapter. An exciting new future awaits you!

14 *Your motivated life*

In this chapter:

▶ you will review the exercises practised so far
▶ you will learn how to maintain your motivation, even when the novelty wears off
▶ you will explore further goal-setting techniques and look to the future.

Achieving your goals is no easy task. It means overriding challenges and pushing forward when necessary. People often find this hard to accept but, in reality, there is no easier option. With practice, however, and using the exercises introduced throughout this workbook, you can acquire the strength you need.

> '*Do not pray for an easy life. Pray for the strength to endure a difficult one.*'
>
> Bruce Lee

In this final chapter, you're encouraged to consider the possibilities. With abundant motivation, where would you take your life?

→ Reviewing your efforts

Let's begin by reviewing your efforts so far. Read through the following list of exercises and make a note of your progress with each one by ticking the appropriate column.

Exercise	I have learned this skill			
	Not at all:	A little	A moderate amount	Significantly
18: Overriding demotivating challenges				
19: Tactical breathing				
20: Tuning into the challenge				
21: Taking action				
22: Quick review				
28: Planning your next actions				
31: Reversing a negative mindset				
37: Dismissing bad habits and excuses				
39: Energizing your emotional mind				
40: Spinning motivated feelings				

Repeatedly using these exercises creates powerful new habits (see Appendix 1 for the preferred order in which to perform them in sequence). They will guide you in positive ways, from making better decisions to feeling confident when tackling major projects. As with all things, your success is simply a matter of practice.

Our plan from here is simple: keep going until you can tick 'significantly' for each skill.

WHAT TO DO NEXT

1 **Keep working through your action plan.**

Don't give up until you achieve the goal you set in Chapter 4. Keep practising the exercises as you go along. You will find the full 'motivation process' set out in Appendix 1 at the back of this book.

2 **Try not to let things slide.**

We sometimes risk drifting away from things; complacency sets in or we start to imagine that it's 'too much hassle'. As discussed in

Chapter 10, keep things in perspective. Your motivation exercises take just minutes to complete.

3 **Once your first goal is complete, set a new one straight away.**

Within six months or so, the techniques in this workbook will be second nature. Your approach to life will change for ever.

→ Secondary goals

'*Arriving at one goal is the starting point to another.*'

John Dewey

Remember: you have been aiming to achieve more than one goal as a result of using this workbook on learning to motivate yourself. If you're still finding things a struggle, consider these factors first:

▶ **Your stress levels**

People find learning new skills stressful, especially when aiming to achieve their goals.

▶ **Your habits**

Demotivating habits are incredibly powerful, particularly when triggered by stress.

▶ **Your mindset**

Do you believe you can succeed? You may be overly pessimistic about your chances.

When combined, these factors create compulsive avoidance. Combat this by mastering the exercises on tactical breathing, dismissing habits and excuses, and reversing negative mindsets. They will clear the way for you to learn other techniques.

IMPROVING YOUR MOTIVATION

If you still find self-motivation heavy going, formally define 'improving my motivation' as a goal. The following steps will help you.

1 **Create a compelling vision statement.** Follow the steps in Chapter 4 to create a compelling vision. Describe the benefits of learning these techniques and envisage a motivated you.

2 **Create a SMART goal.** Follow the steps in Chapter 5 to set measurable targets. For instance, if you set yourself the target of completing each exercise 120 times over the next six months, you're bound to make some progress.

These steps will reconnect you to your reasons for reading this book. Putting it in writing helps, especially if you're struggling. In particular, pay attention to the targets you could set.

FINDING YOUR PASSION

There is another goal to bear in mind: finding your passion.

People succeed because they have enthusiasm. Consider the young footballer who's constantly practising their skills, or the wannabe director, aged 16, who is already shooting film. Such people are obsessed with their compelling vision. It is more than just words; it is passion.

Whatever your compelling vision might be, think about it, read about it, become a little obsessed by it, and *live* it. Passion transforms work into enjoyment. It makes us unstoppable.

PURSUING YOUR SECONDARY GOALS

This exercise takes a couple of minutes. It targets room for further improvement.

 Consider these two goals: improving your motivation and finding your passion.

Write down two things you could do on a daily (or near-daily) basis to progress these goals. Examples include setting targets, reading more and joining a club or social group.

→ I could improve my motivation further by setting the following target:

_____

_____

_____

_____

→ I could increase my passion by doing the following:

_____

_____

_____

Take a moment to incorporate your answers into your action plan. You're not just achieving goals; you're building life skills and finding out what makes you tick.

→ Maintaining your motivation

Let's consider a different perspective. You cannot achieve your 'personal best' every day. Sometimes your efforts will not work out. Occasionally, despite everything you have learned so far, you just won't be in the mood...

There are various reasons for this, and we all have our ups and downs. Unfortunately, these moments steal our desire and then we feel as if 'the novelty has worn off'. In fact, we have lost our motive for action and our goal has become a chore.

Allow yourself some bad days. Pursuing perfection never works. However, try not to lose more than *two days* in a row. The exercises in Chapter 13 will help. Bouncing back turns difficulty into experience, and nothing could be more important.

INSPIRE YOURSELF

People usually hide the difficulty they have with self-motivation. This is understandable; we judge it as a weakness and worry what people will think. Because we are social creatures, other people's opinions have a part to play so, once you're making steady progress, let others know what you're doing. Share your goals, your ups and downs and your evolving approach. People will be more supportive than you may think, and with their support you'll be much less likely to backtrack. Social pressure makes us think twice.

Another approach is to seek out success stories. For example, if you're keen to lose weight, watch TV shows such as *The Biggest Loser*. They teach a powerful lesson: 'If they can do it, so can I', dispelling our limitations in an instant. Other people's success stories can be highly motivating.

Everything becomes easier when we stop trying to go it alone. Try to overcome any reluctance, learn from others and share your experiences.

USE GOAL-TRACKING TECHNIQUES

Tracking your goals means recording your progress. Use a simple one-month-per sheet calendar (downloadable for free from the Internet) and keep it visible. Whenever you hit your targets, mark that day with a note and a tick. For example:

- ✓ Completed two action blocks on the language course.
- ✓ Spent an hour in the gym.
- ✓ Carried out all my work-based tasks.
- ✓ Made motivated decisions around my diet.
- ✓ Spent an hour this morning gardening.
- ✓ Another day as a non-smoker.
- ✓ Revised for five action blocks.

Be honest with yourself – especially if you dislike the results! Accept the reality and consider it a problem to solve. Ask yourself the following questions:

- ▶ Am I finishing my tasks?
- ▶ Do I have a problem when starting?
- ▶ Are negative habits getting in the way?
- ▶ Am I making excuses?
- ▶ Am I thinking demotivating thoughts?
- ▶ Is my mindset to blame?
- ▶ Am I discouraged by anxiety or frustration?
- ▶ Is demotivating behaviour tempting me?
- ▶ Am I complacent?
- ▶ Do I believe in my compelling vision?
- ▶ Is my action plan clear?
- ▶ Am I struggling to feel desire for each action?

Use these simple questions to pinpoint any problems. Refer to your motivation fact sheet and BET records, and pay attention when things go wrong. Once you've identified the problem, the techniques in this workbook will help.

Ask yourself this: 'If I knew I couldn't fail, what would I do?' It's a big question, and perhaps the most important one of all...

⏱ *Exercise 43*

GOOD ADVICE

This exercise takes a couple of minutes. It grants insights into your psyche.

 Imagine you're coming to the end of a long and happy life. You're sitting with one of your grandchildren, whom you love very much. Imagine having some advice to share.

What three important things would you tell them they should do with their life? It could be anything. Write your answers below.

1 _____

_____

_____

2 _____

_____

_____

3 _____

_____

_____

Reread your answers. Most likely, this advice also applies to your life. How can you act on it?

Your life is not a dress rehearsal. What could you be doing with it? Leave the practicalities aside for a moment. Dare to think big and consider these three simple questions:

→ Beyond caring for my children, what important thing could I do with my life?

_____

→ Am I doing it?

_____

→ If not, why not?

_____

· ·

People often give up on their dreams. They think: 'It's impossible! Anyway, I have children now, plus debts and a full-time job...' However, even the largest goal can be achieved when given enough time. It's a question of using your available resources wisely. Unfortunately, people tend to give up too easily.

You owe it to your friends, your family, your children *and yourself* to do interesting things with your life. The exercises in Chapter 2 should give you some ideas. If in doubt, go for something life-changing. (Of course, there must be some balance, but neglecting your own needs is no more balanced than neglecting the needs of others.)

→ Setting big goals

Here are some excellent goals for you to consider:

☐ Learn to meditate

☐ Take up a combat sport or long-distance running

☐ Start your own company

☐ Perform in a play

☐ Get your dream job

☐ Take hobbies or interests to the next level

☐ Become a yoga teacher

☐ Travel around the world with your partner

☐ Write a novel

☐ Learn to surf

☐ Get married

☐ Learn to play a musical instrument

☐ Buy a house

☐ Improve your relationship and friendships

☐ Become a manager at work

☐ Earn a degree

☐ Read the literary classics

☐ Become fluent in a foreign language

☐ Become debt-free

☐ Create a wonderful home for you and your family

☐ Complete a PhD

What goals could you focus on? Come up with three ideas using the space below.

Three future goals I could work on:

1 _____

_____

_____

2 _____

_____

_____

3 _____

_____

_____

Try to choose something exciting! You only have one life, and your time is precious beyond measure. Refer to this list often in the coming weeks.

CHUNKING DOWN YOUR GOALS

Very large goals may seem intimidating, but they're actually quite straightforward when you know how to make them manageable. You simply break them down into smaller and smaller chunks, so that each chunk represents a realistic target to aim for. Here is an example.

Overall goal	*Four years from now: buy my own house.*
Intermediate goals	*Year 1: clear my debts* *Years 2–3: put money away for a deposit* *Year 4: find a house that meets my budget*
Milestone goals	*Year 1: start making better financial decisions; get a part-time job; sell my car*

All goals can be broken into manageable steps like this. In this example, the milestone goals will each take about three to six months to achieve. Once you have identified your milestone goals, you would create a compelling vision, a SMART goal and an action plan for each one.

When faced with a major goal, the first question is: 'How can I break this into smaller chunks?'

HOW TO ACHIEVE ANY GOAL

As a general rule, use this process to achieve any goal:

1 **Know your compelling vision.** Motivation requires a motive. This cannot be just 'a nice idea'. Your compelling vision should create visceral desire.

2 **Turn this vision into a goal (or goals).** Define your goals thoroughly using the SMART goal system. If required, break large goals into something manageable first.

3 **Create an action plan for your goal.** Achieving your goal depends on knowing what to do next. Draw up a comprehensive action plan – it is your roadmap for success.

4 **Map your action plan across time.** Use Exercise 13, 'Mapping your time', in Chapter 6 to decide when to work on your goal. Treat your time with the respect it deserves.

5 **Work on your goal using a next-action list.** Break tasks into manageable next actions and think positively about accomplishing them.

6 **Overcome demotivating challenges.** Bad habits, negative emotions, limiting mindsets and demotivating behaviour all stand in your way. Anticipate these challenges and overcome them.

7 **Desire action.** Understand your action plan and your goal as being the same thing. If you desire the goal, you must desire the action. The exercises in Chapter 13 will help.

8 **Accomplish your tasks.** Whether making positive decisions, accomplishing small tasks, or working for prolonged periods of time – make a start and keep going!

9 **Review your progress.** Track your achievements using a visible calendar, and bounce back from setbacks using the techniques in this workbook.

10 **Keep going until you have achieved your goal!** Practise your new skills, seek inspiration and support, and keep going through difficult times. Achieve this for long enough and your success is virtually guaranteed.

It might seem over-optimistic, but this is genuinely how goal setting works. There are some fundamental truths to bear in mind:

▶ **Carry out enough skilful work to succeed.** This is the only way to increase your chances in life. You have to do the work!

▶ **Learn to enjoy the work you do.** Turn to the PERMA model for help; seek out positive emotions, engagement, positive relationships, meaning and achievement while working towards your goal.

▶ **Resist the urge to do nothing.** Sometimes you will want to slow down or stop, but use your new skills to get moving. Remember, you do not need to feel motivated to act (although relaxed desire does help).

▶ **Refresh your passion daily, but remember rest and play.** Staying motivated means staying passionate, otherwise the 'novelty wears off'. However, remember your need for rest and play – life becomes pointless without it.

By now this should all make sense. What could you focus on next? Are there problems you need to address or life-changing experiences you could pursue? When the time comes, get an exciting plan together and make a start.

DIFFERENT TYPES OF GOAL

Ultimately, motivation depends on our ability to make better decisions. We need to have the ability to:

▶ reject demotivating behaviours

▶ override demotivated thoughts

▶ ease past stress, frustration, and anxiety

▶ see beyond negative rules, beliefs and assumptions

▶ dismiss habits and see through excuses

▶ consider our needs, values and purpose in life

▶ divide tasks into small steps (and think positively about them)

▶ nudge ourselves into action – even if we don't feel like it

▶ recognize our efforts

▶ see our goals and our tasks as being the same thing

▶ amplify motivating feelings in our body.

These skills are vital for achieving a wide range of goals in any of the following categories.

▶ **Habit-based goals**, e.g. keeping a clean and tidy house. These goals are made easier because resistance, habitual avoidance and excuses are easily overcome. Keeping your perspective is straightforward – ultimately they are just small tasks.

▶ **Decision-based goals**, e.g. enjoying a better relationship. Rather than giving in to irrational decisions, our conflicting needs become easier to control. You'll feel better equipped to make motivated decisions.

▶ **Avoidance goals**, e.g. stopping smoking. The skills in this workbook help to tame the frustration and excuses associated with avoidance goals. You'll finally grasp the rewards your goal could bring, and your decision making will dramatically improve.

Summary

You should now have the insights, the tools and the techniques you need to build better motivation and achieve something amazing with your life. Persevere with the exercises and give yourself time to learn them thoroughly. Override demotivating challenges and see the value in taking action. In time, these new techniques will change your life.

It will not always be straightforward, so track your progress and bounce back from disappointments. Perseverance changes everything.

What I have learned

→ What are my thoughts, feelings and insights on what I have read so far?

_____

_____

_____

Use the space below to summarize any actions you identify as a result of reading this chapter.

_____

_____

_____

_____

Where to next?

Stay connected to your passion and remember to rest and play. Good luck!

Appendix 1

→ # The motivation process

The following ten exercises form a 'motivation process' that you can use whenever you need to boost your motivation at will. You will have already come across the exercises in various chapters of this workbook, so they will be familiar, but they are listed again here for ease of reference, in the order in which you should ideally perform them. With practice and repetition, these techniques will form beneficial new habits, and self-motivation will then become a way of life.

 Exercise A

OVERRIDE DEMOTIVATING CHALLENGES

This exercise takes less than a minute. Use it to help you overcome demotivating challenges, whenever you:

▶ are about to distract yourself

▶ are currently distracting yourself

▶ have just distracted yourself.

 Are you avoiding taking action? This is a demotivating challenge. It's created by false messages sent by your brain. Unchecked, it will divert you from your best interests.

→ Breathe in deeply, exhale and *relax*...

→ Accept the reality of your behaviour; identify what you'll lose as a result:

▶ 'I was about to skip the gym rather than lose some weight.'

▶ 'I was messing around on the Internet rather than finishing my essay.'

▶ 'I just avoided calling the bank rather than sorting my overdraft.'

This type of statement dispels any illusions. To confirm the potential negative consequences, ask yourself:

→ Will this make me happy now?

→ Will it make me happy in the future?

→ Is it worth sacrificing my goals for?

Rationally, the answer is always 'no'. This moment is too important to leave to chance.

→ Imagine waking from a trance. If possible, stretch out your arms, take a deep breath, exhale, and relax...

You do not have to give in to every demotivating challenge; you are much more than these signals. You should now feel more alert to such potential challenges. Let's put this new awareness to good use by focusing on what you can do.

TACTICAL BREATHING

This exercise takes 60 seconds or so. It relaxes your physiology, sheds stress and aids rational thought. Use this relaxation technique to enable you to combat demotivating challenges. Read through the steps first to familiarize yourself with them.

Never use this exercise when your full concentration is required, e.g. when driving or operating machinery.

 Look up slightly and close your eyes. Your eyelids might twitch, which is normal. (If you are in a public place and you cannot close your eyes, let them defocus instead.)

→ Next, slowly breathe in through your nose, mentally counting from one to five as you do so.

→ Then exhale through your mouth. Relax your shoulders, jaw, back, stomach, tongue and feet. Tell yourself: 'soften and relax'. Let go of all tension and resistance.

→ Complete ten breaths in total. Be patient, breathe slowly, and avoid 'going through the motions'.

→ If you still feel anxious or frustrated, complete ten more breaths (or more if necessary) until you feel relatively free of resistance.

This exercise just takes moments, so don't rush it – that's the very problem you're trying to overcome! Go slowly and complete all ten breaths each time. Your ability to relax *will* improve, as will your ability to think rationally.

 *Exercise C*

TUNE INTO THE CHALLENGE

This exercise takes less than a minute. It connects you to time, consequence and purpose. Use it before working on your goal.

 In Chapter 2 you completed Exercise 3, 'How much time do you really have?' Look at that diagram now. Accept your time as too precious to waste.

→ Confirm the time and date in your mind. Remind yourself how much time you have left. Remember that you only get to spend it once, and it will eventually run out. So choose wisely!

→ Where are you? What are you here to do? What is your 'motive'? Marry positive action to the present moment, and you'll meet your needs in positive ways.

→ You will encounter demotivating challenges on the way. You may even be experiencing one now, but you do not have to give in to it.

→ How many demotivating challenges might you face today? Anticipate them, recognize them, and ease through them. You'll get more things done *and* be happier in life.

Demotivating challenges are made strong only by *temptation*. Feel certain you'll override them and they weaken dramatically. Remember that we lose motivation when we feel 'in two minds'.

Exercise D

PLAN YOUR NEXT ACTIONS

This exercise takes a minute or so. It helps you plan your 'next actions'. Use this exercise at the beginning of each 45-minute block.

 Note the time and date and read through your action plan. What do you need to do next?

→ Does a time-sensitive task need completing urgently?

→ Is there an order-sensitive task that needs completing next?

→ If not, either select the largest job or warm up first (by completing a few quick tasks).

Note the task and break it into bite-size chunks. Describe *what* you need to do – and *how*. Keep each step under 15 minutes, if possible. Plan for the next 45 minutes or so.

Then organize these steps into the order you'll complete them by numbering each one.

How can you think positively about the work ahead? Try to be specific.

→ Do I need to put it into perspective?

→ What could be enjoyable about this?

→ How can I become engaged with these tasks?

→ Can I 'sweeten the pill'?

→ Can I turn this into a game?

→ Can I create competition?

→ Do I need to boost my energy?

Keep it simple. Try just one or two techniques appropriate for the task(s) you're working on. Take only a moment to sketch out your list.

Exercise E

REVERSE A NEGATIVE MINDSET

This exercise takes a couple of minutes. It will reverse a negative mindset and create freedom. Whereas the other exercises in this sequence are designed for repeated use, you may need to use this technique only once or twice – whenever you feel strongly resistant towards taking action.

For maximum impact, use tactical breathing (Exercise B) first.

 1 Identify your current negative mindset from the list below. If you recognize two or three, choose the one that stands out.

☐ I must not fail.

☐ It has to be perfect.

☐ Things must not change.

☐ I must not succeed.

☐ Pleasure must come first.

☐ I cannot do it.

☐ I am too tired/stressed.

☐ I cannot work like this.

☐ I have plenty of time/I work best under pressure.

☐ I hate being told what to do.

If uncertain, go with 'I must not fail.'

2 How would things change if you adopted the *opposite* mindset?

☐ I'd prefer not to fail, which means staying relaxed and motivated.

☐ Being 'good enough' is okay.

☐ Change is safe.

☐ Success is safe.

☐ Pleasure will come later.

☐ I can get better at this.

☐ I can do this even when tired or stressed.

☐ I'd prefer not to work like this, but I can choose to do it.

☐ My time is valuable/I don't need pressure to perform.

☐ I accept the need to co-operate when it's in my best interests.

3 Describe this new mindset below (or in your notebook). Imagine the thoughts and feelings you'd experience, and the actions you'd undertake. Here are some clues:

→ Feeling calm, happy, relaxed, and focused on your best interests

→ Free from resistance or temptation

→ Aware there is nothing stopping you from acting now

→ Engaged behaviour in the moment

→ Thoughts: _____

_____

→ Feelings: _____

_____

→ Actions: _____

_____

4 Next, we're going to 'pretend' you possess this resourceful mindset. Give yourself permission to do this (sometimes we believe pretending is pointless or forbidden). Allow yourself to use your imagination – it is an incredibly powerful tool.

Put yourself into this resourceful state of mind.

Anticipate feeling different, weird, or 'out of your comfort zone'. This means that the exercise is working.

5 For the next 60 seconds, close your eyes (if possible; otherwise defocus them) and imagine holding this positive mindset.

Stay relaxed and conjure up the thoughts and feelings you'd experience.

Imagine having the freedom to focus solely on your best interests. Let yourself really get into it.

6 Check to make sure:

→ Is this new mindset useful?　Yes/No

→ Will it combat distraction and inertia?　Yes/No

→ Does it open new possibilities?　Yes/No

→ Is it healthy and safe to think like this?　Yes/No

7 If the answer to these questions is yes, continue with this mindset as you work on your goal.

This new mindset should be happier, easier, and more productive than before. Staying positive, relaxed and *free* helps people think clearly and achieve their goals. You have nothing to lose.

 *Exercise F*

DISMISS BAD HABITS AND EXCUSES

This exercise takes just seconds. It restores self-control by dismissing bad habits and excuses. As with Exercise A, use it whenever you are distracting yourself from working on your goal.

 1 Are you experiencing the urge to focus elsewhere? Acknowledge this and state: 'That's just a bad habit created by my brain.' Grasp the reality; there is more to you than this impulse.

2 Did you excuse yourself from working on your goal? Look out for:

→ 'I can't do this, because...'

→ 'I don't have to do this yet, because...'

→ 'It's okay to do this other thing first.'

If you are unsure, ask yourself: 'How am I excusing this distraction?' Acknowledge the excuse and affirm: 'That's just an excuse created by my brain.'

3 Ideally, catch yourself before switching away from your goal. Pause for five seconds, breathe slowly, and relax... If possible and appropriate, sit on your hands – for some reason, this helps! If you've already switched away from your goal, don't worry. Use these steps as soon as you notice. You'll improve with greater awareness and practice.

4 Remember: you do not need to give in to these challenges. Focus on what you *can* do, and switch back to your goal.

Demotivating habits and excuses rob us of our *self-control*. This exercises injects some reality into the situation. Complete these steps and put yourself back in the driving seat.

Exercise G

ENERGIZE YOUR EMOTIONAL MIND

This exercise takes just seconds. It fires up your desire and willingness to act, making action more likely. Use it whenever you want to take sustained positive action.

1 Feeling motivated means holding a desire and willingness to act. To fire that up, scan through your compelling vision statement. Pick out the *words and ideas* that stoke your inner desire. Tell yourself: 'It's okay to want this!'

2 Next, close your eyes and spend 60 seconds mentally 'acting out' achieving your goal. Focus on the ideas and feelings you picked out in step 1. Imagine it vividly; get your emotions going.

Visualizing works by suspending your disbelief and 'pretending' that what you desire is really happening. You don't need clear mental imagery; just *act it out* in your mind. This should create relatively strong feelings.

3 Link the future with the present. Keeping the desire in your body, close your eyes and imagine completing your 'next actions'. Incorporate everything you have learned so far: relaxed action, a clear mindset, dismissing excuses, etc. Understand this: desiring this goal means you *must* desire the next action – even if you cannot sense it (yet).

Recognize that your action and your goal are the same thing. Taking action meets your needs, expresses your values and achieves your compelling vision. Your goal and your action plan are *cut from the same cloth*.

Following these steps links positive feelings to the tasks immediately ahead of you. This should create a desire and willingness to act.

SPIN MOTIVATED FEELINGS

This exercise takes five minutes to learn, and a minute or so to use; practise it often. It amplifies positive feelings in the body, so use it whenever you need to boost your motivation. Read through the steps first and familiarize yourself with them.

1 Focus on your 'next action' now. Think about enjoying the rewards. Vividly imagine your circumstances improving, and feel desire.

2 Observe the feelings in your body, and answer the following questions:

→ What is the location of the desire in my body (stomach, chest, face, cheeks, shoulders, etc.)?

_____

→ How does the feeling move? Is it a rising or a sinking feeling? Is it a tight knot? Does it spin clockwise or anticlockwise? (Feelings move through the body; they pulse, shoot, spin and fizz around. Take a moment to identify these movements.)

_____

→ Does the feeling move quickly or slowly?

_____

→ What texture does it have – smooth, fuzzy, rough, tingly, spiky, no texture?

_____

→ Is it narrow or wide? Is it hotter or colder than the rest of your body?

_____

→ How intense is this feeling, on a scale of one to ten?

_____

→ If the feeling had a colour, what would it be? (Just guess!)

_____

You may need to carry out these steps several times to answer the questions fully.

3 Once you have a handle on the feeling, imagine you can reach into it and push it strongly through your body. Each time you inhale, attempt the following:

→ Imagine growing more determined and motivated.

→ Imagine the feeling moving with greater depth and power.

→ Imagine the feeling growing wider and more intense.

→ If the feeling is moving from your stomach to your chest (for example), push it up and beyond, into your shoulders and your face.

→ Make the 'colour' brighter and more vibrant.

Spend a minute or so moving the motivated feeling around your body. If you lose focus, recall the rewards associated with your goal and reconnect with your desire. Spin it around and amplify it.

Exercise I

TAKE ACTION

This exercise takes just seconds. It re-establishes conscious control, so use it whenever you want to take action.

Begin by asking yourself: 'How does it feel when I *know* I'm about to do something?'

→ Whatever your answer, look at your next task and think, 'That's right! I'm doing that now.' Feel relieved to act in your best interests. Action *is* success.

→ Without thinking or hesitating, nudge yourself forward and start on the task. Keep breathing deeply and stay calm.

→ You may get pulses of hesitation or reluctance. Breathe through it and don't stop. It *is* possible to take action *alongside* the negative emotion. And once started, it's much easier to keep going.

→ Gradually put other things out of your mind and zoom in on the task. Stay relaxed and focused at the same time. Ease past frustration and lose yourself in the moment.

This simple exercise gets us moving. With practice, you will achieve this degree of control within seconds.

Exercise J

REVIEW

This exercise takes a couple of minutes. It reinforces motivation and establishes good habits. Use it whenever you have just finished working on your goal.

Begin by asking: 'What can I tidy up for the next minute?'

→ Spend a little time straightening up in whatever way possible. Keep it in perspective: it's just a single minute.

→ Now update your action plan if necessary. Feel satisfied as you cross items off your list.

→ Program your next goal times into your smartphone or online calendar. Set an audible alarm for each one. This is a great habit to get into.

→ Finally, acknowledge your efforts and the challenges you have overcome – no matter how imperfectly. Try to feel thankful; building motivation is not easy.

Focusing just on results causes problems, as does highlighting our imperfections. Instead, accept that self-motivation is challenging. Feel pleased with your efforts. The importance of this cannot be overstated.

Appendix 2

→ BET record sheet

<u>BET record</u>

Date:

Task:

Part 1: starting on time

Behaviour:
Emotions:
Thoughts:
Habit (Y/N):

Part 2: working on my goal

During: 1	2	3
Behaviour:		
Emotions:		
Thoughts:		
Habit (Y/N):		

During: 4	5	6
Behaviour:		
Emotions:		
Thoughts:		
Habit (Y/N):		

Part 3: taking prompt breaks

Start of break:	**End of break:**
Behaviour:	Behaviour:
Emotions:	Emotions:
Thoughts:	Thoughts:
Habit (Y/N):	Habit (Y/N):

Index